My Wife Wants You to Know I'm Happily Married

AMERICAN LIVES   Series editor: Tobias Wolff

My Wife Wants You to Know I'm Happily Married

JOEY FRANKLIN

University of Nebraska Press   Lincoln and London

Acknowledgments for the use of
copyrighted material appear on page x,
which constitutes an extension of the
copyright page.

Publication of this volume was assisted
by a grant from the Friends of the
University of Nebraska Press.

Library of Congress
Cataloging-in-Publication Data

Franklin, Joey.
[Essays. Selections]
My wife wants you to know I'm happily
married / Joey Franklin.
pages   cm. — (American lives)
Includes bibliographical references.
ISBN 978-0-8032-7844-8 (paperback : alk. paper)
ISBN 978-0-8032-8482-1 (epub)
ISBN 978-0-8032-8483-8 (mobi)
ISBN 978-0-8032-8484-5 (pdf)
1. Franklin, Joey. 2. Fatherhood. 3. Men. 4.
Fathers—United States—Biography. I. Title.
PS3606.R42237A6 2015
814'.6—dc23
[B]

2015021576

Set in Lyon by M. Scheer.
Designed by N. Putens.

For Melissa and the boys, of course.
Where would I be without them?

There is always some madness in love. But there is also always some reason in madness.
—Friedrich Nietzsche

The world has grown suspicious of anything that looks like a happily married life.
—Oscar Wilde

The main thing is to be moved, to love, to hope, to tremble, to live. Be a man before being an artist.
—Auguste Rodin

CONTENTS

ACKNOWLEDGMENTS

First to my patient, supportive family, many of whom have found themselves on the pages of this book, but none more often than my wife, Melissa, and our three boys, Callan, Nolan, and Ian. They are the bright center of everything. I also thank my parents, Rod and DeAnn; my siblings, Krysti, Sherri, Joshua, Misha, Jason, and Tom; and my in-laws, Mike, Cristi, Amy, Caleb, Aubrey, Ross, Natalie, and Chad.

I am likewise indebted to many friends and mentors for their example and writing advice: Patrick Madden, Lance Larsen, Doug Thayer, Dinty W. Moore, Joan Connor, Jill Patterson, Dennis Covington, Kyle Minor, and too many classmates to list. I must also thank those who appear on these pages in pseudonym—those from my past who have the right to remain there if they wish. These are my stories, and I imagine they have theirs.

I could not have completed this collection without generous support from the English Department and College of Humanities at Brigham Young University; the English Department and Graduate School at Ohio University; and the Provost's Office, Graduate School, and English Department at Texas Tech University. I'm particularly grateful to the administrators of the AT&T Chancellor's Fellowship at Texas Tech for their generous funding during my PhD program, where I completed many of the essays in this book.

I would also like to thank the editors of the following publications where my essays originally appeared:

"The Lifespan of a Kiss" first appeared in *Gettysburg Review* 26.2 (Summer 2013).

"Grand Theft Auto: Athens, Ohio, Edition" first appeared in the *Normal School* 1.7 (Fall 2011).

"In Their Ears and on Their Tongues" first appeared in *American Literary Review* 12.2 (2011).

"Climbing Shingle Mill Peak" and "How to Be a T-Ball Parent" first appeared in *Sport Literate* 8.2 (Fall 2013) and 7.2 (March 2012), respectively.

"On Haptics, Hyperrealism, and My Father's Year in Prison" first appeared in the *Pinch* 33.1 (Spring 2013).

"Call Me Joey" first appeared in *Waccamaw* (Fall 2010).

"Houseguest" first appeared in *Mid-American Review* 35.1 (December 2014).

"Language Lust" first appeared in *Florida Review* 35.2 (2010).

"Working at Wendy's" was the grand-prize-winning essay in *Twentysomething Essays by Twentysomething Writers*, edited by Matt Kellogg and Jillian Quint, and originally published in 2006. Reprinted by arrangement with Random House, Inc.

Finally, the three haiku appearing in the last chapter of this book are from *The Sound of Water: Haiku by Bashō, Buson, Issa and Other Poets*, translated by Sam Hamill, © 1995 by Sam Hamill. Reprinted by arrangement with The Permissions Company, Inc., on behalf of Shambhala Publications Inc., Boston MA. www.shambhala.com.

My Wife Wants You to Know I'm Happily Married

The Lifespan of a Kiss

I regard it in the light of a duty to caution my readers emphatically, and at the very outset, as to the danger of even reading about kisses.
—Christopher Nyrop, *The Kiss and Its History*

1. Getting to First Base

It's nearly impossible to tell for sure when the baseball game first appeared in the American conversation as a metaphor for sex, but it's not difficult to guess why it did. How better to describe the frustrations, risks, and rewards of sexual pursuit than to call on the image of a game where going three for ten makes you an all-star? Then there is the game's association with summertime and youthful conquest. The very language and imagery of the game—with its bases, bats, and balls, and its sliding, stealing, and striking out—make it a flexible, if decidedly misogynistic, metaphor. Consider the unintended sexual undertones of this commentary about baserunning in an 1895 issue of *Spalding's Baseball Guide*: "Any soft-brained heavyweight can occasionally hit a ball for a home run, but it requires a shrewd, intelligent player, with his wits about him, to make a successful base runner." And so, let's forget for a moment the glory of a home run, the distance a ball must fly to turn a triple, the hustle and nerve involved in landing a double—forget all of that and instead contemplate briefly the combination of patience, speed, and luck necessary to even make it to first base.

One evening in the thirteenth century, in the secluded study of an Italian castle, Lady Francesca da Rimini found herself sitting alone with her brother-in-law and sometimes-tutor, Paolo. Holding the story of Lancelot and Guinevere open between them, their minds filled with ancient visions of chivalric knights, fair maidens, and rapturous kissing. As such stories go, their "eyes were drawn together, and the hue / Fled from [their] alter'd cheek," and the young Paolo leaned forward and stole a kiss. And, as such stories go, the unhappily married Francesca returned the gesture with gusto. And then as they sat together, lips locked, their book all but forgotten, the jealous husband stormed into the room and dispatched them both with a twitch of his sword.

Such was the lifespan of a kiss for Italian royalty, whose sordid romances involved arranged marriages, drafty castles, and clandestine study sessions. At least that's the storyline Dante wants us to remember. And he should know. He met the couple in the second circle of hell, bound together in a blustering gale of lost souls, eternally damned for one weak moment: an ill-fated kiss.

I hope it was a good one.

What constitutes a "good" kiss, anyway? According to *Princess Bride* author, William Goldman, who claims to have recorded the greatest kiss in history, "the precise rating of kisses" is a "terribly difficult thing, often leading to great controversy, because although everyone agrees with the formula of affection times purity times intensity times duration, no one has ever been completely satisfied with how much weight each element should receive." But let's just say that each element is worth ten points—simple and democratic. Then we get possible individual scores of affection (10) x purity (10) x intensity (10) x duration (10), which gives us 10,000 points—a perfect kiss.

I kissed my wife, Melissa, for the first time while we sat in a small armchair near the front door of the apartment she shared with five other girls during college. We'd just come home from a date, and the room was dark, the apartment quiet, and the chair a little snug for the two of us. The kiss was simple, lingering, electric, and overdue. Five months we'd been dating, and I hadn't kissed her yet (and yes, I know how this will sound to some readers—prudish, old-fashioned, quaint), but I knew when I met her that I might marry her, had an "uh-oh" moment the first time I saw her, actually felt something inside me whisper, "There is the girl you are going to marry." Such romantic notions are fine for the heart, but my brain thought the entire arrangement quite absurd, and so I resolved to pay as little attention to passion as I could so it wouldn't cloud my judgment. Her friends thought we were crazy, and after a while, I'm pretty sure Melissa thought I was crazy. Still, I managed to hold out long enough for my brain to almost completely reconcile itself to my heart, and on that spring night, in the dark quiet of her apartment, I hit a solid single to center field, and the crowd went wild.

2. Seven Minutes in Heaven

Sam wanted to kiss me. Well, okay, not just me, everyone, really. "Greet one another with an holy kiss," admonishes the New Testament four different times, and in Brazil, Sam's home country, they apparently mean it. Sam grew up Catholic and had, at every Mass since he could remember, shared "an holy kiss" with his neighbors as part of the service. So when he met a pair of Mormon missionaries on the street in Japan and agreed to attend a Sunday service, he was disappointed when nobody puckered up. After the service, he pulled me aside and said, with a look of genuine pain in his eyes, "Why no kissing?"

I once attended a Catholic Mass in Beaverton, Oregon, for a friend's First Communion, and at the end of the service, after the torn bread and red wine had passed from lip to lip down the rows of the small congregation, the priest invited all of us to "extend a hand of fellowship" to our neighbors—a firm handshake and the words "peace be with you"—a puritan version of the holy kiss that keeps our friends and neighbors at a safe, sterile distance.

In the Old Testament, God bemoans those who "draw near me with their mouth, and with their lips do honour me, but have removed their heart far from me." What is this but the description of an empty, soulless kiss with all the trappings of passion and none of its substance?

I remember in elementary school how preoccupied I was with the idea of kissing—a preoccupation born, in part, of Disney movies, prime-time television, and the kisses my parents shared in front of us kids. A kiss meant acceptance, affection, and commitment. But I also remember the girls at school brandishing them like weapons, striking at random, and leaving us boys dizzy with the attention, overestimating the meaning of those kisses as much as the girls underestimated their effect.

Rodin's famous sculpture *The Kiss* began life on a main panel of the 1881 version of *The Gates of Hell*, a nineteen-foot-tall, thirteen-foot-wide set of bronze double doors covered in the writhing bodies of the damned—a tribute to Dante's *Inferno*. The embracing figures of *The Kiss* were meant to depict Francesca and Paolo in the consummate moment of their lustful betrayal, and they were meant to feature prominently in the themes of agony and suffering that so dominated *The Gates*. But something wasn't right about the couple, and in subsequent versions of *The Gates*, Rodin relegated them to a minor position on one of the pilasters and eventually removed them from the portal altogether. What was the problem? Their embrace was too pure, their bodies too full of life, the man's hands too hesitant and graceful, the woman's feet all but leaving the ground, the intensity of the kiss lifting her heavenward, ecstatic, rapturous.

3. A Better Fate Than Wisdom

Ryabovitch, the hapless protagonist in Anton Chekhov's 1887 short story, "The Kiss," is an unsociable military officer with rounded shoulders, a long waist, and "lynx-like side whiskers" who finds himself a wallflower at a dinner party full of beautiful people dancing, making small talk, and playing billiards. Looking for an escape from the uncomfortable crowds, Ryabovitch enters what he thinks is an empty, unlit chamber, only to be accosted by a strange woman who mistakes him for someone else in the darkness. "At last," she sighs, flinging her arms around Ryabovitch's neck and kissing him, only to recoil in horror as she realizes her mistake. The accidental couple flees from the room in opposite directions, but the damage is already done. Poor Ryabovitch is smitten.

"His neck seemed anointed with oil," says the narrator. "And on his left cheek, just by his moustache, there was a faint, pleasant, cold tingling sensation, the kind you get from peppermint drops." Throughout the night, he is "gripped by an inexplicable, overwhelming feeling of joy," and the effect lingers for months, distracting him from his duties, filling his mind with irrational fantasies about the girl, about meeting her again, about her perfections, and about the beautiful life they could have together. But as you read on, you realize that Ryabovitch is not so much enamored of the girl but of the kiss itself, the dark room of its genesis, the way it made him feel normal and right and ordinary, and you realize the man has been bamboozled by his own loneliness, deceived into believing that the whole of the world could be found on the soft pout of a woman's lips.

"If you kissed a pretty face, would you not that very instant lose your freedom and become a slave?" warned Socrates. "Would you not have to spend much money on harmful amusements, and would you not do much which you would despise, if your understanding were not clouded?"

A big part of why I waited so long to kiss Melissa had to do with the number of girls I'd kissed before I met her. Growing up, I chased female approval like a starved puppy after a bowl of kibble, and I measured that approval in a girl's willingness to pucker up. For several months in middle school, I chose to forgo the bus in favor of a two-mile walk home beside a girl who would occasionally kiss me before saying good-bye and turning down her street. For half a year in high school, I dated a girl with whom I had little in common because one day she walked up to me in the hall and kissed me on the cheek. And once, I skipped out on work and drove three hours from Portland to Seattle to see an old girlfriend on the off-chance that she might have a few kisses left to give. By the time I'd entered my twenties, I'd kissed so many girls in my search for self-affirmation that I'd come to mistrust the gesture altogether.

"Since feeling is first," wrote E. E. Cummings, "who pays any attention / to the syntax of things / will never wholly kiss you."

4. In a Darkened Theater

I've always sort of known movie theaters were a place that couples went to make out, but I'd never actually seen it until one day in the sixth grade, when I went to a local second-run cinema with some friends. We entered the dark, cramped theater just after the previews had begun and ascended the stairs toward our seats, and that's when we saw them, illuminated by the bright light of the screen—a man and a woman, maybe in their midthirties, embracing across an armrest. One of the man's legs protruded into the aisle as he leaned toward the woman, who leaned in just as aggressively, the popcorn almost falling out of her lap. "The film's barely started," I remember thinking as I took in the image of the couple—their heads rotating comically, their lips crawling all over each other—and I remember feeling in the air something like desperation emanating from their sprawled feet, their pawing hands, and their roving lips, as if at any moment the floor might give way beneath them.

"The real lover," said Marilyn Monroe, "is the man who can thrill you by kissing your forehead."

The 2005 film adaptation of *Pride and Prejudice* has two endings—one for the British market and one for the American market. In the British version, Mr. Darcy and Elizabeth find themselves standing in the misty morning fields outside Longbourn Estate, finally confessing their love for one another. Elizabeth kisses Darcy's hand, and then the couple touches foreheads and embraces in a way that even Queen Victoria could have tolerated. Then we cut to Elizabeth standing in the library before her bewildered father as she explains that she actually does love Mr. Darcy. The film ends with happy Elizabeth leaving her father to ponder over the peculiar nature of romance. "If any young men come for Mary or Kitty," he says, "send them in, for I am quite at my leisure."

The American version adds one more scene, set at some point in the near future, ostensibly on some evening after the wedding. We find the couple in an intimate moment, all the trappings of Victorian propriety removed, with a barefoot Mr. Darcy kneeling beside Elizabeth as she sits on the open-air porch in her nightgown. Torches illuminate the scene as the couple exchanges sweet nothings.

"How are you this evening, my dear?" says Mr. Darcy.

"Very well," says Elizabeth, taking his hand. "Only, I wish you would not call me 'my dear.'"

"Why?"

"'Cause it's what my father always calls my mother when he's cross about something."

"What endearments am I allowed?" he asks.

"Well, let me think," she says. "'Lizzy' for every day, 'my pearl' for Sundays, and 'goddess divine,' but only on very special occasions."

"And—" he pauses for dramatic effect (Mr. Darcy knows what he's doing), "what shall I call you when I'm cross? Mrs. Darcy?"

"No. No," she scoffs in mock disgust. "You may only call me 'Mrs. Darcy' when you are completely and perfectly and incandescently happy." And this is what the Americans in the theater have been waiting for. The couple has been leaning closer and closer together during the entire conversation, and now there's only one thing left to do.

"And how are you this evening, Mrs. Darcy?" he asks, and kisses her on the forehead. He then repeats "Mrs. Darcy" four more times, kissing her on the nose and on both cheeks and, finally, with the firelight reflecting on their faces and the orchestra reaching a crescendo in the background, their lips meet, and they hold their kiss until the scene fades to black.

The only bit missing is the Barry White album and the bearskin rug.

I think we have Lord Byron to thank for the overwrought Hollywood kiss:

They look'd up to the sky, whose floating glow
Spread like a rosy ocean, vast and bright;
They gazed upon the glittering sea below,
Whence the broad moon rose circling into sight;
They heard the wave's splash, and the wind so low,
And saw each other's dark eyes darting light
Into each other—and, beholding this,
Their lips drew near, and clung into a kiss;

Though our first kiss has meant so much to us, if there were annals dedicated to kissing history, I'm fairly certain that ours would not demand more than a line or two: "April 4, 2002: angst-ridden, abstinent couple finally reaches first base in foyer of small Provo, Utah, apartment much to the relief of patient girlfriend. Kiss effectively seals the marriage deal months before actual proposal. Standard Kiss Rating (SKR) based on accepted formula of affection (9) x purity (9) x intensity (8) x duration (7) = 4536 points." A perfectly average, middle-of-the-pack, everyday kiss, much too tame for Hollywood.

5. And They Shall Be One Flesh

There's an unfortunate YouTube video of an unfortunate couple from Portland, Oregon, who made a big deal of waiting until the altar to share their first kiss and then invited a reality TV crew to come to the wedding. What's captured on camera is the entire wedding party looking on as the couple shares a kiss or, rather, a quick series of kisses that make them look a little like two people trying to chew the same piece of gum, or two gerbils trying to drink out of the same water bottle, or, as one YouTube viewer put it, "like a mother penguin feeding her baby." Watching the video, one does not question the couple's sincerity—nor their affection—but their imaginations. So wrapped up in the idea of what they thought a first kiss should be, neither of them appears to have thought about what they wanted it to be, and as a result, they come together like robots, soulless automatons whose fumbling embrace is as embarrassing for everyone watching as it is for them. The camera jumps around the audience, showing what must be siblings, cousins, and parents laughing nervously, averting their eyes, and, one imagines, trying to hold back a gag. The most painful shot shows one of the fathers lowering his head into his hand. "You know it was a bad kiss," wrote one viewer, "when even your dad facepalm'd."

Rodin believed that creativity and sexuality were intrinsically connected and was always trying to close the gap between clay and flesh. He had what one biographer called "the need to touch," and that need manifested itself as much in his romantic relationships as in the "kneading, fidgeting, feeling" way he approached his work.

His first love was nineteen-year-old Rose Beuret, a farmer's daughter who met and fell in love with Rodin in 1864. She posed for him, kept up his studio, and stood with him during the struggles of his early career, but she was eventually relegated to the status of domestic partner, a sort of live-in friend who accompanied him on walks, traveled with him when he wished, and put up for decades with one mistress and casual lover after another—a harem of women that included models, dancers, artists, and aristocrats. Rodin loved women, loved sensuality, and thrived on the creative force he saw emanating from both. So large was the number of women who found themselves entangled in the brambles of Rodin's casual, sometimes-requited love that some observers began to call him a "sultan" and questioned the sanity of his obsession.

As his relationships with women became more complicated, so did his relationship with the female form in his work.

Departing from the relatively tame composition of *The Kiss*, his sculptures became more openly erotic—limbs contorted in a mix of pleasure and agony, lips pressed against bodies, and torsos bent around torsos. Later in his career, he penciled more than seven thousand drawings, described as female bodies "violently agitated either by the memory of, or the waiting for, sexual pleasure." As one critic put it, "Rodin was searching for everything that exalts, maddens, contorts and fevers the human body," and it's easy to see that same searching in his personal life, easy to see how moving from one woman to another, always with Rose in the background, had made some around him uncomfortable. Rose had been his first muse, had helped ignite something inside him, but she'd become little more than a glowing ember lost and forgotten in the conflagration of his search for artistic and sensual inspiration.

On a sunny day in June, a few months after our first kiss, I asked Melissa to be my wife. The proposal should have been an event, a precisely choreographed display of my burning desire for her. I should have traveled across three states as my cousin did when he surprised his girlfriend, hiding in a gift-wrapped box and bursting forth with ring and roses in hand. I should have taken her aloft in a hot-air balloon and proposed, as my friend Tyler did, with the lush Oregon landscape rolling hundreds of feet below him. I should have at least gotten down on one knee. Instead, I forgot to kneel, forgot the clever words I'd rehearsed in my head, and when she said yes, I forgot to put the ring on the correct hand. The entire event proved anticlimactic, and looking back on that scene, I realize I have forgotten nearly everything about the few minutes after my proposal. I know we talked, and I'm sure we kissed, but the words of any conversation have vanished, and the memory of any fevered kiss has disappeared. Certainly, we felt the gravitational shift in our relationship, shared the collective jitters of a "did that just happen?" moment, but the signs of that shift have not survived—no persistent sensation to trigger the memory, no lasting impression, no cool Chekhovian tingling, nothing that lingers in the neurons of my mind or in the memory of my flesh.

A homunculus is a 3-D human model developed by neuroscientists as a visual representation of the way nerves are distributed throughout the body. All the fleshy parts are there as they would be in a real human being, but those parts are either swollen or shrunken out of natural proportion, depending on how much real estate their respective nerves occupy in the primary motor cortex of the brain. So the arms, legs, and torso—areas of simple, coarse movement that require relatively few neural controls—are diminished, while the hands, fingers, and lips—areas of fine, intricate movement that require complex wiring—are exaggerated on a monstrous scale.

To imagine a homunculus walking down the street is to imagine a pitiful creature with hands the size of washing machines swinging at his side, sunken eyes and diminutive nose hiding behind his gargantuan wet lips that protrude forward, flapping as he walks. To imagine a homunculus walking down the street is to imagine private access to the neural preoccupations of a stranger. To imagine a homunculus walking down the street is to imagine witnessing the silent struggle that engrosses each of us every day, a struggle to engage with the world, to manipulate our surroundings, to touch and be touched, to kiss and to be kissed back.

If you flip through our engagement photos, you'll find dozens of images of Melissa and me posing for the camera, doing what engagement photos are meant to do: putting us on display for our friends, smiling at all the people who will send us presents, testing the permanence of the photograph against this new theory of us. And for the most part, the photos do this. Here we are leaning in, our heads touching; there I am cradling Melissa in my arms; here she is leaning over my shoulder from behind. In one, we are lying on the ground beside each other, looking up at the camera with green blades of grass stabbing at our ears, and in another, I'm supporting her as we lean against a gray and brown wall of rock. And then there are two in which we are kissing.

In the first, we are the cute couple that grandmothers and neighbors and my parents' college friends will smile over—the fresh, pure hope for the next generation just a step away from the black tux and the white dress. But in the other, we are something different, and for that reason, it has remained quietly in the back of the album. It's the same photo shoot—we're wearing the same clothes, and the same warm colors of the park fill the background—but I sit slightly behind Melissa, with my face turned toward her as she turns back toward me, and our lips have met, our mouths ever so slightly open, the tension palpable in the tendons of our necks.

We were both startled by the image when we went through the proofs, not because the picture made us uncomfortable, but because it was a snapshot of a side of our relationship we hadn't talked much about, let alone shared with others. This image from a carefully crafted photo shoot designed to capture the prospects of our happy future instead froze in time a rare moment of passionate expression in our otherwise chaste courtship. I remember laughing with Melissa about the prospect of sending off that photo in all of our announcements and the surprise we pictured on people's faces, and I also remember liking the image for its honesty—for its subtle confession that despite the role a traditional wedding has in preserving, promoting, and embellishing certain ideas about romance, chivalry, and purity, at the heart of every love affair is an animal passion that can, and perhaps should, make the outside observer at least a little uncomfortable.

6. Pillow Talk

At nineteen years old, I spent two years living in Japan as a Mormon missionary—long enough to start thinking seriously about what it would be like to date a Japanese girl, even if, as a missionary, I knew I'd never have the chance. I remember wondering how you'd woo a girl in a foreign language, what you might say, how, without a mutual cultural footing, one would even begin to offer a compliment, suggest a date, or steal a kiss. Even after living for two years in the country, my lips could barely manage the language, let alone anything else they might be used for.

Until the U.S. occupation in the 1940s, kissing was not a customary part of romantic relationships in Japan. As a rule, couples did not express affection in public—no hand-holding, no romantic strolls, no cuddling on a blanket in the park. Kissing could get you arrested. Apparently, even in the pleasure districts of geishas and prostitutes, kissing wasn't "part of the repertoire." Considered unsanitary at best and flat-out obscene at worst, kissing was cut from most imported American cinema, and during the lead-up to the war, kissing was derided as an example of rampant Western perversion. In the 1930s, French officials wanted to bring Rodin's *The Kiss* to Tokyo, but Japanese officials would have nothing to do with the now world-famous statue of Francesca and Paolo. To be sure, it wasn't the nakedness of the couple but their mouthy embrace that presented the Japanese officials with such a moral dilemma. Trying to accommodate the French, they even came up with a compromise in which they would agree to exhibit the sculpture as long as they could cover the kissing heads with a cloth. But Paris rejected the offer; morally, the French just couldn't allow it.

During college, a friend of mine named Brandon started dating Nozomi—a striking woman from Osaka with panther-black hair and a name that means "desire." Like me, Brandon had served as a missionary in Japan, and like me, he had zero experience with the Japanese syntax and grammar of relationships. But unlike me, he'd found himself a persuasive reason to learn. Nozomi had lived in the states for several years and spoke fluent English, but her Japanese had the raw, earthy flavor of her native corner of Japan—the interior region southwest of Tokyo that the Japanese call Kansai or Kinki. They dated in Japanese and English, but Brandon was determined to impress her with some of her own dialect. He ordered a book online, and from it he learned to speak with the hypercasual inflection of the region, and the surprise on Nozomi's face the first time he used it was enough to know he'd scored the points he was hoping for. But the book itself, with its red-banded cover and its title in large white letters, proved more of a problem. He read it between classes while attending school at BYU's famously conservative Idaho campus, but he kept the cover wrapped in brown paper, hoping to avoid sideways glances from pious strangers who might wonder about a man reading a book titled *Kinki Japanese*.

The other day, Melissa and I took our children to the park, so they could bounce themselves off the play structure while we chatted in the cool breeze of a spring morning. We wore shorts and T-shirts, and Melissa stood on a balance beam in front of me with her arms around my neck. We stood at eye-level and shared the kind of forgettable small talk born of contentment and the distraction of everyday life. But while standing there in that casual embrace, remarking on the silliness of our boys, the unexpected pleasantness of the weather, and the to-do list of the day that lay before us, I looked at her face and saw her again, as I sometimes do, the way I saw her when we first met. Ten years of life together—a decade made mostly of raising children, paying bills, and folding laundry—all washed away, and the angle of her jaw, the almonds of her eyes, and the soft edge of her no-nonsense beauty appeared at once novel and irresistible to me, and so I leaned in to kiss her, cutting her off midsentence.

She kissed me back in the pleasant-but-impatient way she does when she's in the middle of something and can't understand why I want to stop and kiss her. And I wanted to say in response to her perfunctory peck, "Listen: you are this mysterious creature who surprises me every day, and you make me want to write bad poetry and buy exploding bouquets of purple irises on the way home from work and turn up sappy country music ballads when they come on the radio, and you must know that I love you, and you must know right now, and words are too slow, and not enough, and what else can I do but kiss you?" But instead I said, simply, "Hey, I need a real kiss," and she said back, incredulous, "We're talking," and dismissed my kiss altogether, confused as usual at my timing, unaware that "talking" is exactly what I'd been trying to do.

"A kiss can be a comma, a question mark, or an exclamation point," said Mistinguett, the French starlet who danced and sang at the Moulin Rouge and the Casino de Paris, and appeared in more than forty-six films between 1908 and 1917. She was right about the acute power of a kiss, but it can do more than punctuate: it can apologize, forgive, confess, confuse, demand, offend, remind, embrace, and let go. Each kiss is its own language, with its own set of rules, its own accents and dialects, its own evolution and history, its own risk of growing old, becoming obsolete, and dying off.

7. Not Tonight, Honey

The Kiss is among the most famous sculptures in the world, and yet Rodin thought the couple too "conventional," was displeased with them, and believed the composition uninspiring. "The embrace of *The Kiss* is undoubtedly very attractive," he wrote in 1907, "but I have found nothing in this group." He believed *The Kiss* too formulaic, too scripted. He wanted art to "open up wide horizons to daydreams," and, at least to him, that simple kiss was little more than a highly academic retelling of a tired love story that transcended nothing, and, frankly, he'd had enough of it.

I think it's no coincidence that the punishment meted out to Francesca and Paolo for their illicit romance was to be bound together eternally in perpetual embrace, their passions never forgotten and yet never fulfilled.

Brandon tells me that after he and Nozomi married, they lived in the United States and kissed and held hands in public the way any typical American couple might, but when they moved back to Japan for a few years, things slowly began to change. Each time she held his hand, she felt more and more exposed, and when they kissed, she felt the eyes of every person over forty bearing down on her.

It became too much, and she began to pull away occasionally when he leaned in. Brandon took the rejection in stride though, choosing to tease Nozomi rather than get offended. And now that they live stateside again, they're back to kissing "the way we used to." But Brandon still can't watch a Japanese TV romance without chuckling. "For the entire series, there's no PDA," he tells me, "and at the very end, when a couple finally 'gets together,' they hold hands!" He describes the typical final shot of a couple sitting side by side, interlocking fingers for the first time while they look off into the sunset. His description reminded me that I'd seen shots like that on Japanese television—closing scenes that baffled me, the long shot of the "amorous" couple complete with overdone music and close-up angles of their hands slowly moving toward each other with what, to my American eyes, seemed like all the passion and intensity of a bonsai growth spurt.

Melissa has never been terribly comfortable with public displays of affection. When we were dating, if I pulled her into my arms during an evening stroll, she'd hug me back and maybe even kiss me briefly, but then she'd pull away. Even after we were married, it took some convincing for her to kiss me like she meant it when she dropped me off at work and said good-bye. In a moment of exasperation, I once asked her whose opinion mattered more, the people walking by or mine. She's gotten more comfortable with it over the years, but even around the house, I sometimes feel my homunculus is showing, that I'm all hands and lips and starving for affection, while she seems quite in control of herself, even confused a bit over what all the fuss is about. If passion is an animal best kept on a leash, then hers must trot obediently at her side, while mine drags me tripping and rolling down the street.

Needless to say, she's had some reservations about the writing of this book.

8. The Lifespan of a Kiss

"For a kiss's strength I think," said Lord Byron, "It must be reckon'd by its length."

In ten years of marriage, our first kiss has become one of those moments we relive, the way couples do, tapping into our intimacy archive, trying to rearticulate the past through a sort of living bibliography of the life we're writing together. It's on the top-ten list of our highlight reel, a touchstone for how far we've come, a measure of what we're capable of, and, sometimes, a reminder of what we're missing.

Though Rodin was never pleased with his first version of *The Kiss* and dismissed it as a mere nod to the academy, I wonder whether the sculpture had more personal significance than he let on. Certainly many critics have suggested autobiographical undertones in Rodin's more sexually charged sculptures. *I Am Beautiful*, for instance, depicts a desperate and straining man as he clings to the body of an indifferent, almost disdainful, woman, who appears to be rising up and away from the ground, her face turned away, her body almost out of reach. Another, titled *Minotaur*, mimics the seated position of *The Kiss* but lacks any of the mutual passion. Instead, a half-man, half-bull has accosted a woman and pulled her into his embrace; the wincing woman leans away, repulsed by animal lust. To many critics, these sculptures betray in Rodin an internal struggle about his relationship with women and may suggest that the sculptor was as frustrated and conflicted by his sexual desires as he was inspired by them.

But if that is true, what of *The Kiss*, with its subdued, perhaps idealized, passion? The image is not prudish but reserved and suggests a hint of the sacred, of the intimate and personal. A celebration? Yes, but not a carnival. A burning desire? Absolutely, but not a frenzied lust. If there is an autobiographical hint hidden in that famous embrace, what would it be? A nod to Rose, his first love? To love itself, perhaps, and the simple, seemingly uncomplicated nature of its beginnings? It's impossible to tell, but what's certain is this: *The Kiss* stands center stage at any discussion of Rodin's erotic work—not as his most sensual sculpture but as the genesis point from which his sexual energy emerged.

Of the kissing I did as a child, none of it stands out in my memory as more than self-serving curiosity, and I'm not sure that it would be realistic to expect anything else. It's a Hollywood notion, I think, that as children we can be capable of anything approaching real romantic love. Rather, I think the experimenting I did, that most of us did, was more akin to putting a marble up my nose, punching my sister, and pulling the dog's tail—just one category in a long series of short, clumsy essays in owning a body. Even as teenagers, our kisses can mean only one thing—"I want you, and I need you to want me." And it's becoming clear now that the most significant kisses Melissa and I have shared are the ones that transcend that sense of codependency, the ones least tied to my preconceived notions of passion, of romance, of self-worth, the ones that have opened my mind, as Rodin might say, to those "wide horizons to daydreams" that too often seem unattainable.

There are times when I have wondered why every kiss couldn't be this way, but perhaps I'm coming to know the answer—perhaps a transcendent kiss, like a transcendent sculpture, is not something we decide to create but something we arrive at—that moment for the artist when clay is more than clay, and for the lover when flesh is more than flesh, and for both of them, when the distinction no longer matters.

Working at Wendy's

It's a quarter to nine in the evening, and I'm standing in front of the counter at Wendy's. The restaurant smells of french fries and mop water. In my right hand I hold my résumé. I don't know whether I need a résumé to apply for the Wendy's night shift, but I bring it anyway. It anchors me as I drift toward the sixteen-year-old kid behind the counter and ask to speak to his manager.

"One mandarin orange salad?" the boy asks.

"Uh, no. Actually, I'd like to speak to the *manager*." As the cashier retreats to the back of the store, I recognize a large kid with curly hair working the fryer—he used to play football with some of the members of my Boy Scout troop. He looks up at me, and I avert my eyes. Part of me wants to turn around and leave before the manager comes out. A couple in their twenties walks into the restaurant and stands behind me. I step away from the counter and pretend to read the menu, holding my résumé close to my chest. The urge to leave increases. Just then the manager comes out and asks, "You here about the night shift?"

As I hand the manager my résumé, I realize it is a mistake. He doesn't want to know my service experience, or my academic references, or my GPA. All he wants to know is whether I can spell my name correctly.

"The application is over there," the manager says, handing back the résumé and pointing to a file folder mounted on the wall next to the counter. I take the application to an empty table in the corner of the restaurant and hunch over it, wishing I had a drink, or a hamburger, or something to put on the table beside me.

The next day I go for an interview with the hiring manager. I sit down at a table in the lobby and answer two questions: "What hours do you want to work?" and "When can you start?"

When he was sixteen, my brother Josh got his first job at McDonald's. He lasted two weeks before deciding the greasy uniform and salty mop water weren't worth five bucks an hour. His manager used to show off rejected applications to the other employees in the back of the store. Most were high school dropouts looking for spending money, but a few had college degrees. One application was from a doctor who had recently left his practice because he "couldn't handle the mortality rate."

I think about that doctor now as I sit in a small back room at Wendy's. I have just watched thirty minutes of training videos about customer service, floor mopping, heavy lifting, and armed robbery. Chelsea, the training manager, hands me two neatly folded uniforms and a brand-new hat. Holding the hat in my hand, I look out into the kitchen at my new coworkers. At the fryer is the large high school kid I remember from the night before. A skinny, brown-haired, Asian-looking boy, who must be about nineteen years old, is washing dishes. Two girls are at the front of the store taking orders, and the manager is on the phone with an angry customer. "Can I do this?" I ask myself, and I put on my hat.

Chelsea is pregnant. During our training session, I guess she is about six months along. It turns out she is due in three days. "This is my last week on the day shift," she says. "After the baby is born, I'll be back on nights." This is her first child, she explains, and says she is looking forward to being a mom. She smiles as she pats her stomach and asks about my son.

"Eighteen months," I tell her. "A real handful." I explain that I want to work nights so I can take care of my son during the day while my wife finishes her last semester of college. I ask about the pay, but I already know her answer. "We start at $5.75," she says, "but the night guys get $6.00." I ask her what she thinks about $7.00. She says she'll see what she can do.

Chelsea trains me on Tuesday and goes into labor on Wednesday. I don't see her again for three weeks.

Kile Livingston's mom ran the register at the Taco Bell on the corner of Lombard Street and Allen Boulevard in a poorer section of Beaverton, Oregon. Her name was Deb. She was divorced and had three boys. She shared a three-bedroom apartment with another single mom and her own five children. They listened to Snoop Dogg and Ice-T, drank forty-ounce malt liquors, and walked over two miles round-trip every Saturday to watch the neighborhood boys play basketball at Schiffler Park.

On welfare-check days, Deb went grocery shopping and brought home twelve-packs of Pepsi, stacks of frozen steaks, crinkly bags of potato chips, several gallons of 2 percent milk, and bag after bag of Malt-O-Meal cereal. The week before welfare checks came, they ate eggs and instant ramen—lots of ramen.

Her son Kile was my best friend in sixth grade. We often walked to Taco Bell together to visit his mother. She usually bought us a taco while we sat in a booth in the corner of the store and talked about bicycles, girls, and football. Once, on the way home from visiting his mom, Kile said, "She used to sell drugs, you know. We had plenty of money, and nobody thought she was a bad mom then."

My first night on the job, I work with Dave. He is seventeen years old, five ten, and keeps his hair short, like a soldier. He goes to an alternative high school if he wakes up in time and is looking forward to enlisting in the military when he turns eighteen. His dad, who recently remarried and moved, told Dave he would have to find his own place to live. When Dave isn't sleeping on a friend's couch, he lives in his car—a 1982 Volkswagen Rabbit with a hole in the floor just beneath the gas pedal.

Dave works with me a few nights a week and knows the business well. He's quick with a mop, can make all the sandwiches blindfolded, and has the entire computer memorized. When he's not working, he hangs out in the restaurant lobby trying to steal Frosties and old fries when no one is looking. The manager says she will give him food if he needs it and asks that he not steal anymore. "Asking gets you nowhere," he says, and keeps stealing.

Because I live just two blocks from the store, I recognize a disproportionate number of the late-night drive-through customers. Mostly, I see parents of the Scouts I work with or other Scout leaders and occasionally a friend from school. When they pull up to the window and see me in the Wendy's hat and headphones, the following conversation ensues:

"Joey, I didn't know you worked here! How's it going?"

"Good, good. Just flipping burgers."

"Hey, you gotta do what you gotta do."

Then I explain the job is temporary, and it's the only job in town that allows me to work at night so I can watch my son during the day while my wife finishes school. I tell them in another month I'll be back in school and working at a better-paying, less humiliating campus job.

One evening a fellow Scout leader comes through, and after the typical exchange, he says, "Hey, more power to ya. I know a lot of people who think they're above that." He thanks me as I hand him his triple cheeseburger, and he drives around the corner and out of sight.

At 250 pounds, Danny really fills out his uniform. He played varsity football for the local high school, has earned his Eagle Scout award, and knows his way around a car engine. On several occasions he has changed spark plugs or jumped batteries and has even replaced brakes on the cars of fellow employees, usually right in the store parking lot.

Wendy's is the first job Danny has ever had. With six months' experience, he is the senior employee and is being considered for a management position. He brings in about a thousand dollars a month, much of which he gives to his grandmother. At closing, he always saves the good salads for me and talks the manager into letting me go home early. He likes listening to Metallica, working on his Trans Am, and talking with Tonya, a high school junior who also works at the store.

While I'm washing my hands in the bathroom at work, a well-groomed twentysomething man standing at the sink next to me starts a conversation. "Do you like working the night shift?" he asks.

"It's not bad," I say, shaking my wet hands over the sink.

"How long have you worked here?"

"Two weeks."

"Have you ever thought about college?" he asks. I want to tell him I'm in the top 5 percent of students at my college, that I am two semesters away from graduating, and that I'm on my way to grad school to get a PhD in English literature. Instead, I shrug and tell him the same line I tell everyone: "Oh yeah, I'm just working here until my wife finishes." He doesn't believe me. To him, I look like another wasted life, another victim. He thinks I got my girlfriend pregnant, that I never graduated from high school, that I can't do any better than flip burgers at two in the morning. He feels sorry for my kids.

"I only applied here because I knew I would get hired," says Sara the first night I work with her. She is a nineteen-year-old single mother with a sixteen-month-old boy. She is very tall and wears her long, brown hair in a ponytail pulled through the hole in the back of her Wendy's hat. I ask her why she needed a job so badly.

"I had to get one," she tells me. "My parole officer said it was the only way to stay out of jail." I start at this and then ask, "Why were you in jail?"

"Drugs," she says and pauses, testing me. "I was wearing my boyfriend's jacket, and the cops found a heroin pipe in the pocket." I ask how long she was in jail. "One year," she tells me. "I just got out a month ago."

When I was in fifth grade, my dad got a job delivering pizza. As an eleven-year-old, pivoting on that blurry edge between boyhood and adolescence, I found myself bragging to my friends about the prospect of free pizza and then wishing I hadn't told them anything about my father's job. He worked a few nights a week, and when he came home, his uniform smelled like steaming cardboard and burnt cheese—but he always brought home pizza.

Oren is nineteen years old and works at Wendy's to pay for his cell phone bill and to get out of the house. His parents are devout Mormons and think he is a disgrace to their entire family. He wants to sell marijuana because he believes he can't do anything else. "I don't do anything well," he tells me one night while washing dishes. "I don't know what I want to do with my life." He asks Sara to find some pot for him to sell.

Oren's mother is Japanese, born and raised, and speaks to her children in her native tongue. That means Oren speaks Japanese and has family connections in Japan. Oren also owns an AK-47 and likes to go up into the canyons and shoot jackrabbits. He showed me a picture once of a rabbit carcass, its innards all blown out and dangling for the camera.

Tonight while working the grill, Danny tells me he has never been on a date. "Girls don't like me," he says as he flips a row of sizzling, square, quarter-pound patties. I can tell he believes it. Danny, by his own admission, is the kind of guy girls like for support. He is a gentleman, he asks thoughtful questions, and he's always willing to talk. He thinks his weight and his scruff turn girls off. He tells me he is going to ask Tonya to a movie this weekend but isn't sure she'll say yes. Later Tonya comes into the store, and Danny disappears with her for a few minutes out in the lobby. He comes back with a large smile on his face and says, "I've got a date this weekend. Can you work for me?"

I don't like when Dave works the front line with me. I can't make sandwiches very fast yet, and he gets tired of waiting. More than once he pushes me aside to finish an order. If he sees me hesitate on a step, he barks, "Red, green, red, green! Ketchup, pickle, tomato, lettuce! Come on, Joe, it's not that hard."

Later, while I'm mopping the floor at closing, Dave comes by and takes the mop from my hand. "Like this," he says, scrubbing the tile vigorously. He thrusts the mop back into my hands and walks away, rolling his eyes.

Chelsea is back at work tonight for the first time since having her baby. She appears fairly happy, and I'm surprised at how well she seems to have adjusted to being a working mom. The phone rings several times, and Chelsea takes the calls in her office. She tells me her husband has lots of questions about putting the baby to bed. After the lobby closes, Chelsea disappears into the bathroom for nearly a half hour. This happens every time I work with her. I wonder if she is sick. Then I notice the breast pump in a case on her desk. Another employee tells me Chelsea has been expressing milk in one of the bathroom stalls on her breaks.

Danny and Tonya have been dating for two weeks. He shows up for his shift an hour early to see her before she gets off. They sit in the lobby holding hands and talking for almost the entire hour. When they're not in the store together, she sends text messages to his phone, which I catch him reading while he stands at the grill.

Tonight Danny approaches me while I'm opening boxes of french fries. He wants advice on how to ask Tonya to her junior prom. "I want to do something romantic," he says. I suggest Shakespeare's eighteenth sonnet. He has never heard of it. "'Shall I compare thee to a summer's day? . . .'" I recite. "She'll love it." I print off the sonnet at home and bring it to work for him the next day. He writes it in a card and delivers it with flowers. Two weeks later, in a rented tux at Tonya's junior prom, Danny gets his first kiss.

I call my dad tonight. He asks about school, about my son, and about work. I tell him about Wendy's.

"What? Who?" he says.

"Me. I got a job at Wendy's." Long pause. "I needed a job I could do at night." More silence. "It's not so bad." Still silence. "I work from 9:00 p.m. to 1:00 a.m. a few nights a week."

Just when I think the line must be disconnected, Dad clears his throat and asks, "What happened to your computer job?"

"The guy ran out of work for me."

"Oh." More silence. I imagine he looks around the room to make sure no one is listening before he says, "Wendy's? When did that happen?" I want to tell him that it didn't *happen*, that it wasn't an accident, but I'm stuck wondering how to make him understand and at the same time wondering why I should have to explain anything at all. What would his reaction be if I had chosen to get more student loans instead of the part-time job? I choose to say nothing. Then I offer him my employee discount on fries next time he's in town. He says he'll take me up on it.

When I come into the store tonight, Dave is talking loudly to some employees gathered in the lobby. I ask what all the laughing is about. They tell me that last night Dave and Oren siphoned all the gas out of Dave's stepmother's four-wheeler, and then they urinated on her car door handles.

Everyone dreads working with Chelsea. When she is not in her office counting the till or on the phone with her husband, she sits on the front counter and complains about her mother-in-law. She does very little to help prep the store for closing, and we rarely get out before 2:00 a.m.

Tonight she tells me about her mother-in-law's most recent visit. "I cleaned the house for hours before she came," Chelsea says, nursing a Diet Coke. "And the first thing she says when she gets there is how disgusting the place looks. She won't even eat my cooking." According to Chelsea, her mother-in-law has hated her ever since she got engaged. She wouldn't even visit except that Chelsea has a baby now, and she feels obligated. Chelsea's mother-in-law is disappointed that she is still working. "A mother's place is in the home," she says to Chelsea. "Your kids will be ruined."

Tonight Waymon Hamilton comes through the drive-up window with his family. Waymon lives around the corner from me. His two sons are in my Scout troop, but they spend most of their free time traveling around the state playing premier Little League baseball. They order a few value meals and some drinks, and they ask how I'm doing. There is no hint of concern or condolence in their voices, and I appreciate it.

I hand them their food and watch them drive away. Most

people know Waymon the way I know him, as a dedicated father who works hard at a thankless job to provide for his family. His unassuming nature and warm smile are what I see when I think about him. Few people know him as the fleet-footed running back who helped Brigham Young University win the Holiday Bowl in 1981 and 1983. Few people know he's held several BYU scoring records, including second place for touchdowns in a season, third in career touchdowns, and fifth for both season and career points scored. I didn't even know he played college football until someone mentioned it at a Scout meeting. I once worked an afternoon with Waymon, putting in a new driveway for a neighbor, and he never mentioned his football days once. He told me about his boys, about teaching public school in California, and about pouring lots of concrete.

After the store closes, I come home, take off my uniform, and climb into bed with my wife. She rolls over, tells me she loves me, and murmurs something about the smell of french fries. I kiss her on the cheek and close my eyes. It is winter, but the house is warm. My son is asleep in the next room. There is food in the fridge, and I have a job that pays an honest wage. In the morning I will make breakfast and send my wife off to school. And then, after the dishes are done, if the weather permits, my son and I will take a walk to the park.

Grand Theft Auto

Athens, Ohio, Edition

SHORTLY AFTER MIDNIGHT
Putnam neighborhood · Athens, Ohio

In the silent-street hours of morning on Friday, May 8, 2009, a wanted felon named Craig M. steals a wallet from an unlocked car parked on Lorene Avenue, just a few blocks from my apartment. Lorene runs north and south, skirting the eastern edge of a stately neighborhood with flower-potted porches and brick-paved streets—streets accustomed to the clang of bicycle wheels and the chain-song of dog-walkers; streets sheltered by a canopy of oaks and birches, guarded by the glow of street lamps and the promise of small-town neighborliness—streets completely unprepared for this man Craig, now skulking up the sidewalk, his head down, fingers pawing through a wallet, heart humming with the thrill of the score.

Two blocks west of Lorene, Craig makes a small purchase using a credit card from the stolen wallet. He buys doughnuts, perhaps, or maybe a cup of coffee or a pack of cigarettes. I know he was there because police tell me a security camera trained on the front entrance recorded a grainy image of Craig leaving the store on foot. That's the important detail—"on foot." I can imagine him standing there at the curb, holding a steaming cup of coffee to his lips or perhaps tapping a pack of cigarettes against his palm as he stares out into the darkness. The night is young, and Craig is feeling good, but wherever he goes next, he's going on foot. At this point, he has yet to steal my car.

Putnam Square Apartments #1203 · Athens, Ohio

I turn out the light in my living room and lock the deadbolt on
the front door. I look briefly out the front window at the cars in
the parking lot before twisting the blinds closed and heading
upstairs to bed where my wife, Melissa, lies asleep under the
covers. I'm the on-site manager here, and it's my job each night
to put the apartment complex to bed. I patrol the sidewalks
checking for trash, burned-out lights, and, at least theoreti-
cally, any suspicious activity. But I've been making rounds
each night for nearly a year now, and I've never seen anything
even remotely troubling. This is Athens, Ohio, a small, earnest
Appalachian college town with an enthusiastic Little League,
a teeming farmers' market, and a fifteen-mile bike trail dot-
ted with joggers, dog-walkers, and the occasional recumbent
bicyclist. Sure, it's a party town on the weekends, but people
here leave their doors open, offer rides to strangers, and never
give a second thought to long walks in the evening shade of
all those oaks and birches. One hears about the occasional
assault or robbery, but Athens has no real crime rate to speak
of. The prison isn't much larger than the elementary school.

I climb into bed beside Melissa and pull the covers up to
my chin. Our two boys sleep in the room down the hall, and
outside their window, the glow of a street lamp illuminates the
parking lot like a stage.

1:30 A.M.

Putnam Square Apartments · Athens, Ohio

Craig makes his way east from Lorene Avenue and enters the
quiet parking lot of the Putnam Square complex not long after I
fall asleep. He's from out of state, somewhere in Pennsylvania,
according to police, and perhaps he's just looking for stuff to
pawn—CDs, clothing, maybe an iPod or a cell phone, a wallet

if he's lucky. Then again, maybe he's looking for a quick ride home, his ticket out of town. Or maybe he's heading west, running from Philadelphia or Pittsburgh and whatever trouble he left behind—petty theft, drugs, something more sinister? A part of me wants the man who's about to steal my car to be more than a strung-out addict looking for a fix: a writer of bad checks, maybe, a passer of fake IDs, a wooer of women in every town he comes to. I want him, when he steps through the lamplight of my complex, to feel as though the world is crooked and that he is pulling a straight line through it. I hope, for his sake, that our town feels ripe for the taking and that he feels like more than a just a blip on the quiet calm of this Appalachian spring night.

At the very least, I hope he really needs a ride.

And I hope he has higher standards than to go after my car first. Certainly he tries the handle of the black Explorer parked in front of 708, the one with the wax job and chrome rims. Then the tricked-out Jetta outside 905, then maybe the blue Pathfinder in front of 1202. The Lexus in front of 1204.

Locked. All of them.

It must be desperation, then, that leads Craig to my maroon Ford Escort with the dented quarter panel and dangling bumper. When he lifts the handle, he not only finds the doors unlocked, but by the street lamp's glow I'm sure he notices a camping chair, a folding bike rack, and two car seats. Never mind the interior smells of rotten milk and stale Cheerios; never mind the diapers and fast-food wrappers covering the floor; never mind the cracker crumbs smashed into the upholstery. This car is open, and hey, look there, in the tray beneath the emergency brake—a set of keys.

I imagine Craig turns to the Lexus behind him, and then to the Pathfinder across the way, and then back to my beat-up old wagon, the smudged peanut-butter-and-jelly fingerprints on the back window just now coming into focus.

Does he shrug before he climbs in?

Does he adjust my seat? Put on the belt?

At that moment, asleep in our bedroom, Melissa and I do not hear Craig close our car door. We do not hear the engine start, nor do we hear the fading sound of that engine as our car turns the corner out of the complex, driven away by a determined, if slightly disappointed, car thief who must feel, on the one hand, like the luckiest man in Athens, and on the other, like the butt of some cruel joke.

7:00 A.M.
Putnam Square Apartments #1203 · Athens, Ohio

In the morning, before Melissa or the children are out of bed, I descend the stairs and put on my sandals to take out the trash. The Dumpsters are out my front door, but when I step out onto my porch, I stop, confused by the empty space where my car should be. I look around for an explanation.

I take the garbage to the Dumpster and peer down into the grassy ditch that runs along the back of the parking lot, thinking that I may have left the car in neutral, that it may have simply rolled out of sight. But there are no tire marks in the grass, no car sitting idly in a stream of ditch water. I go back inside.

Upstairs, I wake Melissa to tell her our car has been stolen, and she doesn't believe me. She gets out of bed and repeats my search. When she cannot find the car, she pauses in the living room, realization dawning over her, and then she says, "Do you think someone's playing a joke?"

MIDMORNING
Unknown location · Athens, Ohio

Where Craig takes our car first is unclear. We can extrapolate about Friday's events using clues he leaves behind in the car after it is recovered by the police:

One O'bleness Hospital discharge bag,

One O'bleness Hospital water jug,

Several items of clothing, including a gray sweatshirt and a white tank top,

One hairbrush,

One bottle of lotion,

Two cigarette lighters,

A gas can containing three gallons of gasoline,

One iPod charger,

One Ford factory alloy wheel, originally attached to the car, but apparently removed by Craig and replaced with the spare,

Approximately 100 small white tablets of Oxycodone in a prescription bottle, written for a woman named Colleen, and

One empty can of Coors Light.

Here's my hypothesis: Sometime Friday morning, while I'm busy on the phone with the police and my insurance company, Craig uses our car to pick up a woman named Colleen from the local hospital. She has apparently been in long enough to need a change of clothes, a hair brush, and, as soon as she gets out, a cold beer.

9:15 A.M.

Putnam Square Apartments #1203 · Athens, Ohio

Standing in my living room, dialing my insurance company's phone number, I do not feel as though my single-most valuable possession has been stolen. Nor do I recognize the irony that this beat-up Ford sits atop my "most valuable possessions" list. Frankly, I don't feel much of anything. I should be frantic. Furious. I'm a graduate student working three jobs to support my family, and some freewheeling opportunist just drove off with our only vehicle. But I don't feel any of those things. If I feel anything at all, it's a mixture of curiosity and pity.

Who would steal our car?

Our Ford is on its fourth engine and second major accident. We've replaced the timing belt, the alternator, and another thousand dollars' worth of miscellaneous engine parts. We've even joked about leaving it on a street corner somewhere overnight with the keys in the ignition. Of course, we'd never really do that, but now we don't have to.

The insurance agent on the phone tells me the car will have to be gone for a month before they'll pay out on a claim. I tell her we're hopeful the car will turn up. I tell her we feel stupid for leaving the keys inside it, that it's just not like us, that we can't believe our luck. Then I hang up and explain the situation to Melissa, who is looking out the window at the empty space in front of our apartment.

"Well," she chuckles, "I guess it's time to go car shopping."

MIDDAY
CVS Pharmacy · Athens, Ohio

Craig and Colleen stop by a CVS Pharmacy sometime on Friday to fill the prescription for the Oxycodone. Then they head north on State Highway 33 toward Columbus. I am surprised at the sheer quantity of pills in the prescription when I later find them in my car. The bottle gives off a satisfying rattle when I pick it up.

At some point that day, Craig removes our bike rack from the back of the Escort. It is never recovered. Also unaccounted for when we retake the vehicle are the fold-up camping chair and a few dollars' worth of McDonald's gift certificates that we'd been saving in our glove box for the occasional drifter holding a sign on the highway.

I like to think that Craig and Colleen stop at the McDonald's on Highway 33 just outside Columbus and use our coupons to order double cheeseburger meals with large Cokes. I want them to ask for extra tomato and to go back for refills. I hope that Colleen doesn't, in the silence of waiting for their order, ask Craig about the car he's driving but instead tells him how glad she is to finally be out of the hospital.

They probably talk about hospital food as they eat, making jokes about green Jell-O and tapioca pudding, and Colleen laughs as she places a french fry in her mouth, savoring the salt, distracted momentarily from whatever part of her that still hurts.

Perhaps Craig came to Athens to meet Colleen—an old friend from Pennsylvania? A cousin? A lover? Maybe he found out her discharge date and came to surprise her. Certainly the car had been a surprise—child seats in the back, a sippy cup rattling around the floorboards.

Maybe after lunch, Craig tells Colleen the car belongs to a friend, and maybe Colleen believes him. Or, more likely, she tries to ignore what she has already figured out: this is not some friend's car, and they're going to be in trouble. Real trouble. She wants to say something, but instead, she stands out on the curb in the McDonald's parking lot, smoking a cigarette while Craig pulls the jack from the back of the car.

4:00 P.M.
Ohio University · Athens, Ohio

At school, the car theft makes a great story. My students laugh for five minutes. They know what my car looks like, and they accuse me of orchestrating the whole thing. Friends pat me on the back and offer rides. Melissa sends me a text with links to minivans on eBay. We chat online about car loans and insurance payouts and resale value and down payments. I allow myself to imagine driving a new Mazda5 or a Honda Odyssey. We chat off and on for an hour about new cars, and then I remember our old one has been gone less than a full day.

"Maybe the car will turn up," I write. It seems like the right thing to say. The honest thing. But even as I type it, I don't want to believe it.

"Yeah," Melissa writes back after a long pause. And then she changes the subject.

EARLY EVENING
City limits · Columbus, Ohio

Sometime Friday evening, Colleen and Craig pick up a woman named Brenda, and to make room for three, Craig must do something about the car seats. I imagine that after driving all day in my car, Craig has adjusted to his unfamiliar surroundings. He's figured out the sticky brake, the unresponsive accelerator, and the buttons and knobs for the air-conditioning. He definitely changed the radio presets to all the local rock stations, and his cell phone is charging on the floor. But maybe what he can't get used to are the car seats in the rearview mirror. Sure, I can believe Craig is okay with the idea of me standing on my porch in my pajamas and scratching my head—the sucker who left his keys in his car—but I want to think it's harder to laugh off those car seats and the kids who will no longer use them.

And maybe Colleen finally spoke up. She is glad to see him, and she is glad for the ride, but frankly, she can't believe what he's done.

"What if we get pulled over," I imagine her saying, her elbow propped up on the armrest, her forehead in her palm. "You'll go to jail. We'll go to jail."

I see Craig shrinking in his seat, in my seat, feeling stupid for not thinking all this through. I can see Colleen ripping into him about rash decisions, about putting himself first, about the car seats in the back of the car. Craig hollers something about picking her up, wanting to see her, something about ditching the car as soon they can. Colleen takes off her gray sweatshirt and throws it in the back. I see her reaching around one of the car seats to her hospital bag and pulling out a large white bottle of pills. She unscrews the cap, pulls out a few tablets, and pops them in her mouth, downing them with a drag of melted ice from the bottom of her Coke cup still sitting in the holder. Colleen tosses the bottle of pills toward the back of the car and curses. She pulls a cigarette from a pack tucked in the console beneath the emergency brake and lights it. She inhales deeply, holds in the smoke, and then rolls down the window to exhale. The air around them fills with the whoosh of the open window, and then they are quiet.

Perhaps picking up Brenda creates a welcome shift in the mood inside the car. Perhaps Craig is grateful for an excuse to take one of those seats out and put it in the way back, glad to unbuckle the other one and push it over onto its side, out of sight.

9:00 P.M.
Putnam Square Apartments #1203 · Athens, Ohio

We're not even through our first day as victims of grand theft auto, and we've already stopped using "if" in our car-shopping discussions. The police have told us that ninety percent of stolen cars are recovered in the first seventy-two hours or they're not recovered at all. And if they do recover the vehicle, they're pretty sure they'll find it in a ditch somewhere out in the country, abandoned after some alcohol-induced joyride. Of course, someone could sell the car piece by piece, but considering its condition, my money is on the joyride theory—the car thief tearing up the highway toward some wild deep of West Virginia or disappearing down some Kentucky dirt-road hollow, leaving nothing but a trail of cigarette butts and empty beer cans behind him.

Yes. I'm sure of it. The car is gone, already buried hood-deep in some backwoods bog at the end of a long rutted road to nowhere, and we'll never see her again.

We put the kids to bed and spend the rest of the evening looking up cars online. One particular van, a red Mazda5, has caught our attention—low miles, straight body, and clean interior. But what really gets us is the price—nearly $3,000 less than every other comparable model. Then Melissa notices why. At the bottom of the page, in small print, are the words, "Salvage title: theft recovery."

11:55 P.M.
Downtown · Columbus, Ohio

Just before midnight, Brenda is driving our car with Colleen in the passenger seat and Craig in the back when she makes a right turn without signaling and nearly hits a patrol car. I don't know why Craig has invited Brenda to drive—perhaps Colleen didn't want to sit by him anymore; perhaps Craig has been thinking about his fight with Colleen and about rash decisions and jail, and maybe he thinks he knows a little about the laws governing grand theft auto, and so he intentionally puts someone else in the driver's seat. Maybe he's been drinking—maybe they've all been drinking—but I imagine the moment he sees the red and blue lights reflecting off the dark interior of the car, he regrets letting Brenda get behind the wheel. Either way, during the routine traffic stop, the officers run the car's plate, discover it has been stolen, and, as they say, the game is up. For all of us.

When questioned about the car, Brenda points to Craig in the back seat and says something about the car belonging to one of his friends. Brenda is arrested for possession of a stolen vehicle. Craig is arrested for his implication in Brenda's story. Colleen is not arrested, but the car is impounded, and she has to find her own way home without the prescription drugs, hairbrush, sweatshirt, and everything else in the back of the car.

Our Escort sits on the side of the road, leaning slightly on one spare tire as it waits for a tow truck, its only passengers the two upturned car seats in the back.

SHORTLY AFTER MIDNIGHT
Phone call · Athens, Ohio

A few minutes after the arrest, a Columbus police officer sends a text message to the Athens City Police Department. The officer on duty calls to give us the good news. My wife and I are in bed when the phone rings.

The officer informs us that our car has been found and tells us to call the station in the morning for instructions. I hang up the phone. We both sit up in bed and laugh. Losing our Escort was like losing the family pet—if the family pet were an incontinent mutt with fleas and a penchant for vomiting on the carpet.

We were sad to see it go.

But not really.

And now we were happy to get it back.

But not really.

MIDMORNING SATURDAY
Police impound lot · Columbus, Ohio

Saturday morning I call Officer Filar of the Athens City Police Department, and he gives me the address to the Columbus impound lot where my car has been towed. In this conversation, I first learn about Craig, Colleen, and Brenda and the circumstances of their arrest. I'm surprised to get names and brief histories from the officer, surprised at how quickly my mind gives imaginary faces to these people who've been driving my car around, and surprised at how giving them faces makes them suddenly unsavory.

A little after nine, I catch a ride with friends to the impound lot and spend two hours standing in lines, filling out forms, and talking over the phone with a representative from my insurance company who is very glad to hear that our luck has changed. I end up paying fifty-five dollars to get my own car out of impound.

From the bizarre collection of personal items I find inside the car, it appears that Brenda, Colleen, and Craig had assumed possession of the vehicle and, in essence, moved in. I clean out the car and leave everything that doesn't belong to me with an officer at the impound lot. I climb in the driver's seat and turn the key and, for the first time, begin to feel something akin to loss. It's a weary, disheveled confusion, like someone has been in my bed without my knowing it.

1:45 P.M.
AutoZone · Canal-Winchester, Ohio

I stop at an AutoZone on my way back to Athens, so I can replace the spare tire with the wheel in the back of the car. At this point, I still can't figure out why Craig removed it, and I'm here to buy an air-pressure gauge to see if it's flat. I've gone from feeling violated to feeling annoyed.

Standing at the AutoZone counter, I share the events of the day with the cashier: a short curly-haired woman with the chapped hands of a mechanic. She thinks Craig probably removed the wheel to sell it. She tells me this as if it's the most obvious explanation in the world, as if any other explanation is ridiculous, as if she can tell that I'm one of those guys who probably deserves to get his car stolen.

She's right. The tire isn't flat.

Craig must have wanted to sell the wheels but didn't want to drive up to a pawn shop in a stolen car. If he'd found a buyer, would he have removed all four wheels and left my car cut off at the knees in some back alley, resting on its own knobby axles?

As I jack up the car out in front of the AutoZone, I imagine Craig doing the same thing with this same jack less than twenty-four hours earlier. Maybe someone even stopped to help, or at least offered him a "tough break, man," as they walked past. Craig would have nodded and smiled, maybe said something offhanded about the car always giving him trouble.

"But hey," he might have said. "At least she runs." Kneeling against the car in a parking lot, or on the side of the road, arms twisting the long, awkward crank of the jack, Craig would have looked like any other person replacing a flat tire. He would have looked just like me.

My last stop before driving home is a car wash down the street from AutoZone. I know it's probably just in my head, but I feel as if I can taste other people in my car. The air smells of cigarette smoke, and the press of strange bodies seems to linger in the upholstery. My son's peanut-butter-and-jelly fingerprints are still on the window, but those prints are covered by the prints of strangers now sitting in jail somewhere in Columbus.

I throw away garbage and vacuum the floorboards. I reprogram the channel presets on the radio. Under the back seat, I find a large, gray sweatshirt that stinks of tobacco. I don't want to know who it belongs to. I set the shirt in the way back and return to cleaning. I wash the outside of the car and then look at the wheels. Their spiral grooves are always dirty, stained brown with road grime. I hate these wheels because they're so hard to clean. I laugh at the idea of Craig trying to sell them. Five minutes of scrubbing with the foam brush, and they're still dirty.

After a final rinse, I wipe down my Escort with clean towels from the car wash and look at the wheels one more time. If Brenda had remembered to use her turn signal, I might not be standing here staring at my car like it's some kind of infected sore. Craig, Colleen, and Brenda might have gotten to wherever it was they were going, and my wife and I might still be car shopping. Later, when this is all over, I will want to imagine the rest of their histories I didn't get from Officer Filar—I'll want to get inside their heads, to taste their motives, to play out how all this went down, to pass out the benefit of the doubt like candy.

In this moment, though, I just want a clean car.

I reach inside the back of the car and pull out the abandoned, gray sweatshirt. Carefully, I roll one sleeve around my hand and crouch down next to a wheel. The brown grime comes off easily on the cotton knit, leaving behind silver metal. When all four wheels are clean, I wad up the sweatshirt and throw it into a garbage can. And when I do, I think about the people who spent an entire day in my car, and I feel a little guilty, as if I've just stolen someone's shirt.

In Their Ears and on Their Tongues

The Japanese verb "to bless" is an unfortunate mash of voiceless palatal and velar consonants that staggered and tripped across my tongue the first few times I tried to say it. *Shukufuku.* It didn't matter where I put the stress—whether cramming the consonants together ("shkufku") or giving each syllable its own beat ("shu-ku-fu-ku"), the word sounded hopelessly profane to my nineteen-year-old ears. Kneeling in a classroom full of other new missionaries preparing for a two-year trip to Japan for the Mormon church, I bowed my head and listened as one of us tried to piece together the simplest of Japanese prayers. I knew the *shukufuku* was coming, so I bit my lip and held my breath. But when it finally broke on my ears, I broke into a fit of giggles, and so did everyone else.

It took weeks to get through a day's worth of prayers without chuckling, an educational obstacle made worse by the fact that we'd begun joking around with the word: "Do you smell that? It smells like *shukufuku* in here," or "Oh, dude, you just stepped in a huge pile of *shukufuku!*" We had no linguistic history with *shukufuku*, no semantic cords we could use to strap it down, and so it free-floated in our ears, a kind of verbal inkblot. It shouldn't have been so funny, but with the pressure of our pending twenty-four-month mission and with the nine-week crash course in a language that sounded like an angry sushi chef chopping onions, I don't see how we ever could have said the word without ginsuing it, and ourselves, into a thousand pieces. Still, we were missionaries—future teachers and representatives of our church and, as we saw it, of God—so we had to learn to pray, *shukufuku* and all.

At the end of most days, after baths and pajamas and stories, I kiss my two older boys good night and remind them through the darkness of their bedroom to say their prayers. My six-year-old, Callan, a veteran, kneels on his bed, pressing his elbows into his pillow, and mumbles quietly to himself. Nolan, his three-year-old brother, a rookie, lies face up on his mattress and shouts back across the darkness for help.

Nolan knows the posture, and he knows the verbiage, but he gets a little stage fright. With some encouragement, he rolls onto his knees and folds his arms beneath him. I imagine he thinks this is all a game, more than routine and less than ritual—important enough for Dad to repeat with him every night, but important, why? I coach him line-by-line until he takes up the prayer and runs with it. Sometimes he gives thanks for his dump truck, sometimes for his "bum." Sometimes he asks for a blessing on his brother, other times for a blessing on his blanket. Always his prayers are sweet, innocent offerings of childhood curiosity, testing the limits of his toddler lexicon as he learns to feel out the practical boundaries of Providence.

After more than two months of training, I'd learned just enough Japanese to make me dangerous on a crowded street in Hiroshima. And that's exactly where I ended up, standing on a street corner in a dark suit and tie, passing out pamphlets, eager to use my "*sumimasen*" and my "*hajimemashite*" and my "*yoroshiku onegaishimasu*" on anyone with a few moments to spare. Most people walked on by, but a few usually stopped, and someone occasionally agreed to meet for a lesson.

We taught prayer first. A simple lesson—speak from the heart, move from gratitude to requests, and close in Jesus's name. Things to remember: humility, faith, reverence. Things to avoid: vain repetition, vain repetition, vain repetition. Most had never said a Christian prayer, and so they spoke in tentative, nibbling expressions, an unsure curiosity in their tremulous voices. Watching this struggle, I mistakenly assumed that prayer was something new for them, something foreign, as if each of them hadn't been born with a prayer in their ears and on their tongues, as if the notions of gratitude and supplication spelled out on my flip chart were some grand Western revelation, instead of an elemental description of what it means to be alive.

I learned to pray at home, kneeling on our living room carpet, surrounded by four brothers and sisters who all bowed their heads, arms folded—some against the couch or coffee table, others bent over on the floor. My father either asked one of us to pray or simply bowed his head and began. His voice, normally casual, took on a professional affectation that reminded me of a message left on someone's answering machine—perhaps a formal request dialed in to the department of human affairs, maybe an automated call center for the needful soul. For heartache and pain, press 1; for confession and council, press 2; for grace and general thanksgiving, press 3; for life-threatening emergencies requiring immediate response, press 4; all other supplications, please stay on the line.

The windows of my first apartment in Japan faced the rising sun as it crept upon us each morning, steaming us alive as we lay atop our stifling futons. Even at six thirty when the cool air still clung to the asphalt outside, the room grew hot and humid. I lived with three other missionaries then, and every morning we opened our windows to cool the apartment while we studied. The man who lived beneath us also opened his windows to let in the same cool air, and it was from this man that I heard my first Buddhist chant. While I sat on my floor studying Japanese grammar and preparing lessons, my neighbor's incantations came in through our window as a low mechanical buzz, but soon I recognized the voice buried beneath the sustained, monotone rhythm. The sound carried for sometimes twenty minutes without interruption, riding the morning air like the vibration of a bass string pulled taut across the mouth of a steel barrel. And that sound brought with it not an air of gratitude, confession, or supplication, but of simple being—a hum that said, "I am."

As a child, I wanted a miracle, a life-changing vision, a sea-splitting, dry-ground moment of divine intervention.

What I got was a baseball. My brother's, actually. I'd taken it outside to play without permission, and somehow, in the yard, it took a wild bounce and disappeared. I looked under bushes. Under the car. In the gutter. Nothing.

My brother was going to kill me.

I went into my parents' room and knelt at the foot of their king-size waterbed—the closest thing in our house to an altar.

It took only one prayer.

I went back outside and glanced around the yard. The baseball sat waiting for me in the middle of the street.

Miracle? It was no burning bush, but for a five-year-old, it was good enough.

A few months after I arrived in Japan, my father visited me on the way home from a business trip in Singapore. We had plans to meet for dinner at the chapel near my apartment in a town called Fukuyama, about two hours east of Hiroshima. He came in from the airport by train and got in a taxi at the Fukuyama station. My father spoke no Japanese, and the driver spoke no English, and though I'm sure my father pronounced the name of our church to the driver in that slow, deliberate way some people do when faced with a language barrier, the driver had no idea where my father wanted to go. Instead, he put the taxi in gear and drove my father to the only part of town he could imagine a lonely, middle-aged American man would want to go.

The night club district where the driver let off my father was only a few minutes from the church, but with no cell phone, no map, and no Japanese, my father could do little more than stand on the curb holding his coat, wondering what to do next. Not-yet-drunken pedestrians milled past him, bowing their heads under doorways lit by neon bulbs, and above him, a web of power lines and rising buildings blocked out the night sky.

Two men in dark trench coats stood by the door of a night club, eyeing my father. Then one of them crossed the street and, in broken English, tried to ask him where he wanted to go. With hand gestures and a few words, and maybe a silent prayer or two, my father explained that he was looking for a pair of missionaries. Fukuyama was not a large town, and even night-club bouncers in Japan know a little English, so at the word "missionary," the man reached inside his coat pocket and pulled out a pamphlet I'd given him on the street sometime earlier that week. The man called another taxi, and within a few minutes my father arrived at the church to meet us for dinner, carrying with him a folded pamphlet and a story he would tell over and over again in years to come, wearing it out like an old, tired prayer.

My mother's prayers with the family, no matter how simple, were always loaded. She prayed with the voice of an overworked parent raising five kids on welfare food and the doubtful promise of latchkey child care. She punctuated her prayers with an occasional exasperated sigh, tearful supplication, or thinly veiled bit of counsel directed to her listening children. She did not merely pray: she cried, called, inquired, sought, knocked, asked, beseeched, petitioned, supplicated, implored, entreated, and sued. No request was too big, and none were too small.

She prayed for the sick neighbor and the cold stranger. She prayed for our leaky roof, for our unpredictable carburetor, for our empty bank account. Then she got up off her knees and baked bread for the neighbor and opened our house to that cold stranger. She put buckets under ceiling drips, borrowed a car from a friend when the carburetor finally quit, and drove that car to work, where she turned out regular sixty-hour weeks—each stamped timecard a petition and a promise.

Japan is a nation of workaholics—a nation where coming home at six thirty in the evening is considered "cutting out early"—a nation where commuter trains are packed like last-minute luggage, where a train station marks the flow of people coming and going like the confluence of two great rivers. My fellow missionaries and I used to wade out into this stream of tired, work-weary commuters, trolling for the teachable, not because we thought the fishing good, but because the barrage of rejections we inevitably encountered was, in our minds, a sort of circuit training or mental conditioning—a way to toughen ourselves up, thicken our skin against the reality that few people were biting on the line.

I spoke to thousands of people on the street, asking in my most polite Japanese whether they didn't have a minute to talk. And I received the full run of generic excuses—I'm late, I have to work, I'm Buddhist, I'm going to miss my train, maybe next time. Some people merely gestured politely, holding their palms together at their chest in apology, or not so politely, waving a hand in my face as they walked by. But occasionally people got creative. More than one man told me it was not our fate to meet. A woman hunched over a walker once told me she was too old to talk. And one man—a particularly bedraggled commuter—stopped dead in his tracks, looked at me, and asked, "God? You want to talk about God?" Then he looked at his watch, glanced ahead to the station, and turned back to me. "I know God," he continued. And then he put his finger to his chest. "I am God. Me. I'm all the God I need."

I believe that everyone prays, whether they know it or not. What is a love letter, after all, but a prayer to Beauty? A cast ballot, but a prayer to Democracy? A farm loan in west Texas, but a prayer to The Soil? Even the rage of a drunken boyfriend, a doped-up mom, a desperate suicide bomber, is a kind of dumb prayer—a blind supplication, a cry for help. Human nature compels us to reach out, to look for anchors that moor our lives against the rocking, churning deep. It is for this reason that gods are, as a rule, jealous, for if a person can find lasting meaning in what they can see in the world around them, what need do they have for a God who remains invisible?

All children in Japan learn to place their hands together in prayerful reverence over a meal they're about to eat. The proper approach is to bring your palms together, fingers pointing upward, hands close to the chest, and bow your head as you recite one simple word: *itadakimasu*, which means, more or less, "thank you for the meal," "I do not deserve it," and "I will partake of it humbly." The prayer ascends to God, or descends to the soil, or simply floats in the air for the cook.

I have seen this offering in restaurants, at schools, and in people's homes. I've seen it used as a joke, the comedian saying "*itadakimasu*" as he pretends to put something inedible—dog poop, a shoe, a small kitten—into his mouth. Members of my church, who offer a Christian prayer over their meals, still bring their palms together after the "amen," adding Eastern closure to the Western ritual. But there was something compelling about those little children, the way they closed their palms over their bowls of rice, parroting their parents to be sure, but at the same time trying out the first comprehensible bits of a new language.

I envy the sweetness of a child's prayer—what a more jaundiced person might call naiveté. But I think there's a reason a preteen Jesus was found teaching the elders in Herod's temple, a reason Krishna often runs through paintings with the dimpled thighs of a toddler, a reason the Dalai Lama is tapped as a small boy. Consider my son Callan, who listens to the world around him and prays accordingly with little time for doubt, or skepticism, or any concern for scale. Once after playing all morning in the living room with NPR running in the background, he prayed, "Please bless the people who can't pay their mortgages, and bless the people who need health care and taxes and stuff like that." During the summer Olympics in 2008, he offered this prayer over breakfast: "Thank you for the food. Thank you for all our blessings. And please bless Michael Phelps to win ninety-eight gold medals."

Shinto shrines, with their quiet, manicured gardens and aging gates of wood or stone, are ubiquitous in Japan, often crammed between tall buildings or skirting the edge of some rural rice field—tiny islands of tranquil spirituality. Many sell small wooden placards upon which devotees may write their prayers. The placards are then hung on a wooden stand near the sanctuary—posted so that gods, the universe, and a curious missionary might take notice.

I once visited a shrine shortly after *Shogatsu*, the busy New Year's religious holiday, and read some of the placards left by the crowds. "Please help me to pass my entrance exam." "Please help so and so come home from the hospital soon." "Please bless my son while he is away at college." "Please help me find a good job." Individually, the prayers rarely reached beyond the generic, mundane supplication, but all together, they swung heavily on that wooden stand, weighed down with the collective hopes and desires of an entire community—an outward symbol of their conviction, as substantial as their many footprints still pressed into the drying mud.

I know the Bible says to pray inside my closet, but the teacher in me wants my boys to see Dad roll out of bed in the morning and onto his knees. Still, I know what the Good Book says about hypocrisy, too. I fear they'll notice that some mornings I fall asleep drooling onto the comforter—that some mornings, some days, even some weeks go by where I forget altogether. More than that, I'm afraid that with a front-row seat to my life, they'll catch me in the inevitable hypocrisy of the prayerful: that we often ask for precisely the blessing we aren't willing to create on our own—a peaceful home, comfort to suffering friends, an end to hunger, help for survivors buried under the rubble.

Around my one-year mark in the country, I spent my day off with a small group of missionaries at Hiroshima's Peace Park and Memorial Museum. The park, an expanse of winding concrete paths and rolling green spaces, was constructed at the hypocenter of the 1945 atomic bomb explosion and consists of one emotionally draining memorial after another. At least five monuments honor the thousands of schoolchildren who were in class when the bomb struck, two sculptures show women clinging to the bodies of burnt and mangled children, and inside the museum proper stand two wax sculptures—a woman and a child shown staggering through a bomb-blasted street, their skin melting off their bones, their eyes and mouths disappearing into blackness. If I had been a parent then, the images would have been too much. As it was, I could barely stand the thought of all those bodies burnt, lifeless, and wasted.

But at one memorial, the scene was different. A solitary young girl stands in stone atop a large, three-legged conical monolith. The girl's arms are outstretched, and above her head flies the wire silhouette of a giant paper crane. The girl,

Sadako Sasaki, was only two years old when the bomb went off, and she lived a mile away from the hypocenter. She and her family survived the initial bombing, but over the next decade, Sadako would grow ill and eventually die from fallout-induced leukemia.

Sadako folded more than one thousand paper cranes while she sat in her hospital bed, an act of faith in an old Japanese legend that promised the folder of a thousand cranes a single wish. Though Sadako died, the crane has become a symbol of peace in Japan and Sadako a symbol of all the children killed in the bombing. Young students from all over the country send folded cranes to her memorial in Peace Park. And as a result, nearly every day, the stark granite sculpture of a girl whose prayers went unanswered is flocked by thousands of small, winged offerings.

My oldest brother, Josh, is not a praying man. Not even remotely. "Parents shouldn't teach their children anything about religion," he has said on a number of occasions. He believes that children should be allowed to grow up free from the influences of religion until they are old enough to make decisions about spirituality for themselves. He believes the religion he and I were exposed to as children threatens to make us anxious, repressed sheep with persistent guilt issues. Parents, he believes, have no right to indoctrinate their children. He has turned away from what I have turned toward, and I believe we are both operating under the same risky impulse—the impulse to pray: mine, a prayer to faith, divinity, and the risk of trusting everything to God; and his, a prayer to logic, humanity, and the risk of trusting himself over everything else.

I was once given a small Buddhist prayer book by a man on the street who had no desire to hear my message but appreciated the worn soles of my missionary shoes. Inside the book were the words to the chant I'd heard through the balcony window of my first apartment in Japan. "*Nam Myōhō Renge Kyō*" is the superlative chant, or sutra, of Nichiren Buddhism and sings of taking refuge in the sublime law of life, the supremacy of cause and effect, the value of a chance meeting on the street. In quiet moments, I have incanted the mantra, felt its words reverberate in my chest and out through my fingertips, creating a visceral sense of giving myself over to something. Leaning, groggy, into my comforter in the morning has never done that, even at its best moments.

Over the radio one day recently, I heard a brief news update about a six-year-old boy who'd accidently gone aloft in his family's homemade hot-air balloon and was, at that moment, floating some 2,000 feet above Fort Collins, Colorado. Perhaps it was the thought of my own six-year-old trapped in a home-made balloon, perhaps it was a lack of sleep, perhaps it was my own stupid willingness to believe what people tell me, but tears welled in my eyes for that little boy, and I prayed. It didn't occur to me to drop everything and say a prayer when I heard news of the tsunami in Indonesia. It didn't occur to me to pray when Katrina hit New Orleans. Nor did I pray when just a few weeks ago, I got an urgent e-mail about my grandmother's impacted bowels and the surgery that she might not live through. No, it took that balloon boy and his self-promoting parents to write a fiction absurd enough to knock me out of that momentary sense of control that keeps us all above the surface most of the time.

When I found out about the hoax, that the balloon was a publicity stunt for the parents fishing for a reality TV show, I wanted to recant my prayer, to spit it out like a brown, moldy bruise on the inside of an apple. When I heard that the parents could be charged with felonies and thrown in jail, I was pleased, relieved even. And then I thought about their son, who had been manipulated into believing that the prospects of money and celebrity were worth lying for and who might have to watch his parents go to jail, and I found myself again feeling prayerful for the boy trapped, not in a balloon, but in a family.

The promises of prayer that I believe in, that I spent two years teaching people about in Japan, promises about uncovering truth and overcoming trials and finding comfort—they did not pan out for Kumiko. Her son had been killed in a car accident, and she wanted answers. Why had her son been taken from her? Where did he go? Would she ever see him again? Kumiko's husband had witnessed the accident, but the shock of it kept him from coming home that night. He couldn't face his wife with the news. Kumiko waited and waited for them to come home, and finally she called the police and found out that her little boy was dead.

The people around Kumiko reached out with religion. One friend introduced her to a pair of Jehovah's Witnesses. A family member called the local Buddhist priest. A neighbor invited her to come speak with my companion and me. For weeks she met with all of us, separately. She prayed, read scripture, meditated, and sat quietly while priests chanted sutra and burned incense. But the words and the prayers and the smoke merely floated above her head and filled the room with contradictions and dead ends.

Week after week, nothing we suggested and nothing she did seemed to help. I was twenty-one by then, near the end of two years of teaching people that God loves us and that he answers our prayers, and I found myself standing before this tear-stained woman with absolutely nothing to offer. I'd prayed enough in Japanese by then for the silliness of *shuku-fuku* to be replaced by a genuine sense of supplication. I could feel in the words of a Japanese prayer the same comfort and clinging that I'd always felt in English, but I did not know how to make that true for Kumiko. Where I had merely faced a language barrier, Kumiko faced a great numbing wall of grief. We met a few more times, but eventually she decided to move on alone.

A few days after our last meeting, my companion and I rode our bicycles out to her house and left a loaf of bread and a sympathy note on her doorstep—two small prayers against our failure.

The other night, Callan came out of his room and stood in the hallway, holding his ratted, plush Labrador under his arm, both his head and the dog's cocked awkwardly to one side.

"I'm scared," he said, his lower lip quivering. I put my arm around him and walked him back into his room, listening as he explained why the dark was too dark and why he was sure his doggy would come to life and maul him in the night. While Nolan slept in his bed across the room, Callan went on and on about the darkness, exhaustion and imagination both tugging at his mind. I forced myself to resist the urge to stop him, to slip into a litany of parental platitudes—there's nothing to be afraid of; it's all in your head; just close your eyes and forget it; look, your brother's not scared.

Instead, I asked him a question:

"What can I do?"

When he was smaller, he often wanted me to lie down beside him or sing him a song or turn on the hall light, but on this night, he looked up at me, dog in hand, and said, "I want you to say a prayer to make the earth spin faster so it's morning sooner."

What could I do? This should have been my time to explain that not all prayers are answered the way we want them to be, that God's will trumps our own, that God can do anything but that doesn't mean He will. I knew the darkness of Callan's bedroom was nothing, but to his six-year-old mind, the night he wanted gone, the shadows he and I could do nothing about, were everything.

I think I pray because life has, since I was young, always seemed like a series of intermittent moments of control flanked by persistent suspicions of utter powerlessness, and I want to believe in a power outside of that system, a power capable of righting the boat, of writing the happy ending. But when I think about Kumiko, I wonder whether I have ever really prayed at all. I've known prayers to be euphoric, meditative, confessional, cathartic, lyric, and even revelatory, but I've never faced the lifeless body of my own son lying in a morgue. At the very least, I want prayer to be a stop-loss option against existential crisis—but when that crisis comes, will prayer be enough?

Perhaps, if I am unlucky, my boys will have to face such a crisis first. And perhaps that is why I watch them fold their arms at the table before meals and listen as they give thanks for the steamed cabbage and lentil soup; maybe that's why I kneel with them in the living room and help them ask for help with the spilled milks and scraped knees of their young lives; perhaps I'm training myself as I train them to bow their heads in their seats and ask for safety before a long car trip.

They pray now for the same reason they brush their teeth and remember to flush the toilet: we have taught them to. And we keep reminding them. But eventually when they pray, they will hear not our voices in their ears, but their own; and regardless of any answer they do or do not receive, those prayers will ascend from their tongues like tiny flares, intimate bursts of color against the darkness, a signal of something in the distance waiting to be discovered.

Climbing Shingle Mill Peak

They who come rarely to the woods take some little piece of the forest into their hands to play with by the way, which they leave, either intentionally or accidentally.

—Henry David Thoreau, *Walden*

A red biplane came upon my troop that morning in a slow, quiet grumble, like some late-August thunderhead rolling out of the west. An airplane was the last thing we had expected to encounter on our hike, me and the motley pair of Boy Scouts who had reluctantly followed me up this mountain. But there it was, sputtering in our direction, cutting a noisy line across the sky toward us. We were on the second day of a two-day hike that I'd hoped would provide some cheap wilderness enlightenment, but until that moment, you would have thought the boys, with their cast-down heads and shuffling feet, were marching to their deaths. So when I saw that small plane coming right at us, and saw the boys standing speechless on the path behind me, I allowed myself a little hope. Our hike was nearly over, and I was becoming desperate for these boys to feel something, anything, out here on this windswept ridge—and I thought maybe this plane would come with some meaning mounted on its wings, thought that maybe it would wake them up to the wild earth as it slipped around them on all sides.

We had paused for a water break on the western saddle of 10,690-foot Shingle Mill Peak, an inconsequential mole on the spine of Utah's Wasatch Front. We were on that mountain as part of Operation On-Target weekend, a high-adventure Scout program developed in the early 1980s that challenges troops to first reach a mountain summit and then use signal mirrors to communicate with other troops on nearby peaks. In years past, Scout troops on key western peaks have relayed signals from the Lewis Mountains of northern Montana to the Huachuca Mountains of southern Arizona. With the full light of the sun, the metaphor-laden experience can teach boys the power of direction, patience, faith, and timing; it can unplug them from their wired lives for a weekend and let them feel the alpine wind on their faces as they grow smaller and smaller in the ever-widening expanse above the timberline. It's a chance to get out and discover that the top of a mountain can be a personal, triumphant place.

We began our trip on Friday afternoon, turning off the highway and striking up the side of Squaw Peak Ridge on the narrow paved road into Rock Canyon, which turns to gravel as it leaves the grizzled crest and descends into the green. From the valley suburbs, the Wasatch Mountains look ragged, brown, and foreboding, but concealed within their granite walls is an oasis of aspen, fern, and wildflower; a lost world of snow-melt photosynthesis; a High Uinta Eden crawling with cougars, bears, and rattlesnakes. I pointed all this out to the Boy Scouts riding in the back of the truck as we dropped into the canyon, told them about the snake I saw a few weeks earlier curled in the grass beside the road, and showed them the bite kit I'd bought for our trip. One boy smirked and wanted to know whether I thought the rain would let up. The other boy, who'd been staring out the window, turned to me with a blank look and shrugged.

We parked the truck in the deepest draw of the canyon and started our climb. Behind us lay an abandoned, overgrown campground, and ahead of us ran five miles of narrow trail leading to our summit. For nearly three hours the boys marched behind me with their heads down, grumbling through rain-soaked underbrush and stands of quaking aspen. They wanted to break every ten minutes to lean their packs against the trees, sip Gatorade, complain about wet socks, and ask whether we could stop for the night. By the time we pitched our tents in the grassy meadow below Shingle Mill Peak, they were so tired, bored, and bothered that they just wanted to eat and go to bed.

"I went to the woods because I wished to live deliberately," wrote Henry David Thoreau in an early chapter of *Walden*, "to front only the essential facts of life, and see if I could not learn what it had to teach, and not, when I came to die, discover that I had not lived." With a borrowed ax, Thoreau spent the spring and early summer of 1845 felling trees, splitting logs, and notching mortise-and-tenon joints to build himself a cabin on the shore of a small lake near Concord, Massachusetts. He brought bread and butter for lunch, wrapped in his daily newspaper, which he read while he ate, his pitch-covered hands seasoning the meal with a slight hint of pine. I imagine that flavor was part of the answer Thoreau was searching for—one of the essential facts of life that could ward off the fear of never really living. As a Scoutmaster in my midtwenties trying to motivate a handful of teenage boys, I spent much of my time experiencing this fear on their behalf because they so rarely seemed concerned about anything at all.

I began working with the Boy Scouts in my neighborhood during my sophomore year of college. There were six of them: Bronson, Brian, Serge, Tyler, Landon, and Leo. As a young husband with a small boy of my own, I imagined working as a Scoutmaster would be practice for raising my own son, a way to escape to the woods myself, and a way to pass on some of my own hard-learned "essential facts."

We met every Tuesday in a room off the gymnasium at our church, and though a few of them wore their uniforms, brought their handbooks, and earned their share of merit badges, most just liked to camp, as long as camping didn't interfere with their social lives. They listened to Ludacris and Nelly on their iPods, played basketball and Xbox till all hours of the night, and drank Mountain Dew by the liter. At our weekly meetings they leaned back in their chairs and looked sideways at each other, waiting for me to finish my lesson about plant habitats, wilderness survival, or proper flag folding. The basketballs were always out before I could say, "Dismissed."

This trip was supposed to be a game changer—a motivational gauntlet that would bring them one step closer to manhood. Our narrow strip of suburban Utah shouldered up to some of the most magnificent mountain terrain in North America, and while we'd been out there to camp in the past, we'd never hiked a summit. This was an opportunity for the boys to feel the sheer size of a mountain, to check themselves against a wilderness that civilization only thinks it has conquered. I wanted the boys to "get in touch" with nature in ways they hadn't before and, in so doing, get in touch with themselves—discover a way to look at the world from the canyon side of things.

At our Tuesday meetings, the boys even seemed relatively enthusiastic. Together we chose a peak, reviewed backpacking essentials, made our own signal mirrors, and in the church parking lot learned how to aim those mirrors from one mountaintop to another using a compass. We went over and over what to bring (extra socks, rain gear, sunscreen) and what not to bring (iPod, Game Boy, Mountain Dew), and the night before the trip, I called each of them to double-check that they'd be ready. The next day, a half hour after we were supposed to leave, only Landon and Serge had shown up. Tyler had forgotten about football, Bronson and Leo had overlooked family activities, and Brian had just plain forgotten.

When I turned seven, my mother took me to JCPenney to buy my first *Cub Scout Handbook*. I was about as tall as the glass counter, and while Mom talked to the clerk, I peered inside the display case. I saw a stack of pinewood derby cars, a pyramid of blue Cub Scout mugs, and a brown, flat-brimmed Smokey the Bear hat. There were gold-colored pins and steam-pressed uniforms, rows of merit badges, a pair of hiking boots, and even a Swiss Army knife with a fold-out screwdriver and bone saw. I was hooked. I wanted to be the Scout on the cover of *Boys' Life*, gazing intently at my leader as he revealed the mysteries of the compass. I wanted to sleep in a tent pitched in a row of identical canvas tents, stand and salute the flag with a dozen other boys in green shorts and knee-high socks, and march single file into a wilderness that would teach me how to be a man. I wanted the Norman Rockwell Scouting experience. I doubted my Boy Scouts even knew who Norman Rockwell was.

The older of the two boys on the trip, Serge, hadn't earned a merit badge or rank advancement in two years, but he came on almost every campout. He was the second oldest of four brothers and the oldest at home. His single mother worked at a local nonprofit dedicated to helping Hispanic immigrants adjust to life in the United States. Serge volunteered there occasionally, cleaning and helping his mother run errands. For our summit hike he wore a pair of baggy jeans and unlaced basketball shoes, and for food he brought a foot-long hoagie and a sixer of Gatorade. Every trip he hiked slowly, ambiguously, as if he didn't know or care where he was going, and he almost never said a word. When he did speak, it was with an archer's caution—quiet, well-aimed, and deliberate.

The younger boy, Landon, on the other hand, had a Kalashnikov approach to conversation. I met him shortly after moving into the neighborhood, and he invited me on a camping trip before I'd even volunteered with the troop. He talked all the way up the trail that night, peppering Serge with questions, jokes, and hardy slaps on the back. Serge remained quiet, mostly, and the two of them were in their tent shortly after dinner, asleep before the sun went down.

For all his volume, Landon was much more than just a talker; he was the real Scout in our group. In addition to collecting a slew of merit badges, he had earned his Life Scout, the second-highest rank for boys, and he attended almost every activity. He spent summers on staff at organized Scout camps and served in the Junior ROTC program at his high school. Still, I couldn't even convince Landon to stay up long enough to see the stars come out. Instead, while the boys climbed into their tent, I sat up with the fire, drying our wet socks and shoes for the morning hike. Around me, 50,000 millennia of granite glowed pink in the sunset. Aspen leaves shimmered in the wind, and the cold breath of the mountain sighed down the canyon walls. Eventually, the alpine cathedral paled, faded, and disappeared into the darkness. Clouds rolled in, their low, gray canopy blocking out the stars, and as I zipped myself into my tent, the wind picked up, drowning out the sounds of the night, leaving me alone to wonder—and worry—about the morning.

It was the solitude of Walden Pond that Thoreau valued most: "I have, as it were, my own sun and moon and stars, and a little world all to myself." Yet his small world was little more than a story he wrote down—a lie he told himself to make his narrow patch of woods feel more substantial. His hunt for the essential facts required a certain amount of alone time with nature to be sure, but with Emerson's cabin just a mile away, the rail line and a neighbor's fence visible on the horizon, and visitors stopping by more than occasionally, meditative solace must have been hard to come by. I can't fault his desire to get away, though. Thoreau recognized better than most the sedative effects of modern life, and he recognized the power of the wilderness to rouse us from our sleep.

At seven the next morning, I rousted the boys, and we went over our plan: eat breakfast and hit the trail by eight thirty, so we could be on our peak by eleven. Landon and Serge shared a Pop-Tart on the other side of the fire ring and half listened as I recapped the details. I told them about the American flag stuck in a rock cairn at the summit and a canister there for hikers to leave notes in. I reminded them about the other troops that would be on Mount Nebo to the south, Mount Timpanogos to the north, and Mount Goshen to the west. I held up one of our homemade mirrors. If the clouds cleared, I explained, we'd be reflecting sunlight in their directions by lunchtime. The boys looked like they might climb back into their sleeping bags. I told them to pack up, and while they broke down their tent, murmuring about the clouds and the shortage of Pop-Tarts, I turned the mirror over in my hands, trying in vain to catch some kind of signal.

We could have purchased survival signal mirrors at an outdoor store for less than ten dollars, but we chose to make them out of scrap instead. We got small pieces of mirror from a local glass company and used screwdrivers and files to scratch out pea-sized sight holes in the center of the gray reflective backing of each piece. Then, aligning the sight holes, we glued two pieces of mirror back to back, creating a double-sided mirror with a solitary sight hole at its center.

To cast a signal, you first stand so that you are facing both your light source (usually the sun) and your target. Then you hold the mirror up to your dominant eye with one hand and look through the sight hole at your other hand as you raise it out in front of you, fingers extended in a peace sign. Next, you sight your target through the crosshairs of your outstretched fingers. To capture the necessary light, you simply rotate the mirror in the direction of your light source and watch through the sight hole for a reflection of light to appear on your raised fingers. The distance your signal will travel depends on two things: the strength of the light source and the clarity of the air.

One Tuesday night, using a high-powered flashlight and their mirrors, all six of my Scouts discovered how the right mixture of geometry and patience could produce strong signals across the gymnasium, on the ceiling, and in each other's eyes. Each was eager to try it out on the mountaintop. That morning, as we made our final preparations for the climb, I worried that even if the sun did come out, there might not be a great metaphorical moment for anyone. I worried we might hike for hours and come home with little more than the dirt in our shoes—that our proximity to nature had tamed it, rendered a ten-thousand-foot peak a mere sideshow, a distraction, a checkbox on a long list of things we really ought to do.

From our base camp, the trail to the peak took us out of the thick underbrush and onto a windy slope that led to the slowly rising saddle ahead. Below the trail, the canyon opened up to reveal a tiny sliver of the valley floor and a hint of graying civilization. I wondered to myself whether the boys had noticed that the larger trees had given way to a scattering of juniper bushes and alpine grass growing in the washes beneath us. I wondered whether they had noticed the deer droppings or the snake's burrow just off the trail. We were stepping into the dizzying skyline at more than 9,000 feet above sea level, and I wondered whether they could, in this quiet, sense our distance from the valley floor and its everyday bustle—their entire world reduced to a vanishing point on a landscape canvas. Perhaps they had noticed. Perhaps they had looked over their shoulders, down the slope of the canyon, and were feeling something. I decided to ask them.

"What are you thinking about, boys?"

Landon laughed. "When I get home, I'm going to take a shower and play my Xbox all night." Serge just wanted to know how much longer we'd be.

I decided to stop asking questions.

On my first overnight backpacking trip as a twelve-year-old Boy Scout, I ran caboose in a line of a dozen other twelve-year-olds up two and a half miles of switchbacks and undulating trails to a small lake stocked with rainbow trout. We hiked in a blinding downpour all afternoon, and when we finally arrived at camp, we rushed to pitch our tents. Abandoning our ambitions for a fire and a fresh-fish dinner, we lay in our soaked sleeping bags, an inch of water pooling in the bottom of our tents, and ate cold hot dogs as we shivered and cursed the Scoutmaster who'd brought us out there. As an adult, though, I think back on that trip, and what comes to mind is not the wet socks and the cold, sleepless night but how fog lifted off the lake in the morning and how my friend, standing alone on the sandy lakeshore, pulled taut a fishing line as a rainbow trout arced out of the water. I have painted that scene in my mind the way I imagine Rockwell would have—subtle, idyllic, and unabashedly sentimental. I believed then in the mythology of the woods, that they would offer their own brand of salvation from the dangers and pitfalls of the world, that an important part of who I am as a human being could be found only outdoors—and I still do, though I was never sure how to make that rub off on my Scouts, especially the ones who couldn't be bothered even to show up. What's worse than a boy too busy to sleep out under the stars? Perhaps a boy who comes out under those stars and finds no reason to search them for answers.

Thoreau cultivated a distaste for time, for the economy of schedules, and the waste of men's minds to the business of making money, of making small talk, of making things. Rather than allow work bells and dinner parties and "petty pleasures" to drag us from one end of the day to the other, Thoreau would have us live "as deliberately as Nature." But how does one keep time like the migrating swan, gather food with the cautious tenacity of a grazing deer, ride the current like a fallen leaf, observe the sky like a quiet mountain?

The deepest thinker of my Scouts, Leo, chose to spend the weekend with his dad. Leo's parents had been separated for more than two years, and his mother worked full time to take care of him and his younger brother and sister. I always had mixed feelings about his absence on a camping trip. Leo complained about any type of work, whether washing dishes or pitching a tent, and he often scrapped with the other boys. Once he argued with Landon for an entire evening about who should go collect firewood, and they ended up eating a cold dinner. At the same time, though, in that rare quiet moment around the campsite, when he thought no one else could hear him, Leo opened up. He asked about my child, my wife, and my career plans. He told me about the motorcycle his father would buy him, the trips they would take, the fun they would have.

In between campouts, Leo often stopped by my house unannounced. I could always tell that he wanted to talk but didn't always know what to say. Instead, he offered to walk my dog, mow my lawn, and hold my son. One day I asked him about school. Leo always refused to read during Scout meetings, and I knew he had trouble with vowels. I knew that he attended a special literacy class once a week and that reading frustrated him. I asked him to bring a book the next time he came by, and, to my surprise, he did. Three times a week we met together to read. I wrote vowels on notebook paper, and we practiced. Dog, hog, jog, log. Book, cook, shook, hook. We read from a simplified version of *Journey to the Center of the Earth*. He forced the vowels to make sense in his mind. He was asking questions, making progress, and learning to read. At least, that's what I wanted to think. Instead, our tutoring sessions piddled out after less than a month. The copy of *Journey to the Center of the Earth* sat on my bookshelf, waiting for him to come get it.

We reached the mountain saddle at a quarter to ten. For the first time we could see beyond the canyon wall to the east. The Rocky Mountains spread out beneath us, rolling toward Wyoming and Colorado. For miles in that direction we could see few signs of human life. Behind us, to the west, the grid-lined streets of our hometown sprawled across the valley and disappeared into the shallow waters of Utah Lake.

We sat down on some rocks to drink. The boys sagged with exhaustion. Clouds were still blocking the sun, and I was beginning to fear a revolt from the boys, who leaned against each other, staring at the ground.

Norman Rockwell's Scoutmaster makes it look so easy—tending fire under starlight as the dozing heads of Scouts peek out of pup-tent flaps; raising a red-sleeved arm in thoughtful gesture as neckerchiefed young boys hang on his every word; pointing the way forward at the head of a smartly dressed troop of boys armed with bedrolls and great open-mouthed smiles. In my favorite image, Rockwell's Scoutmaster stands, clipboard in hand, fielding questions from a tenderfoot at his side, while boys lowering a canoe into the water behind them wave energetically at a group on the opposite shore. And in the foreground, a younger Scout kneels at a fire and offers a ladle of something hot to a fellow Scout, who bends low and sips from the spoon—no Pop-Tarts in sight.

Our water break on the saddle lasted longer than usual. Behind us lay the trail that wound down and back into the meadow where our tents were pitched. The boys seemed to lean in that direction as they sat on the ground, waiting for me to give the word. Ahead of us waited the final mile and a half—a poorly marked ascent across large, unnatural ledges cut into the side of the mountain. These ledges, so large and permanent that we could see them from the valley floor, are actually erosion terraces carved out by the Civilian Conservation Corps in 1933.

That year, Utah County had an unemployment rate of more than thirty percent, and the average income was less than a dollar a day. The Civilian Conservation Corps brought hundreds of young men, many just a few years older than my Scouts, up into this canyon and others like it, not for exercise and enlightenment but for the dignity of a pay stub.

That same year, Norman Rockwell painted a calendar portrait of smiling, saluting Boy Scouts from all over the world—hopeful, youthful faces with eyes only for the future. Rockwell's painting, titled *An Army of Friendship*, was inspired by the 1933 Boy Scout World Jamboree held in the forested hillsides outside Budapest, Hungary. Both the painting and the Jamboree seem to throw themselves in the face of the global economic crisis of the time. Nearly 26,000 Boy Scouts from around the world converged on the Royal Forest of Godollo for two weeks of living in the woods with other uniformed boys, trading patches, tying knots, and playing field games—two weeks of trying to discover something essential about themselves, despite the chaos and uncertainty around them.

But in Utah, so many thousands of miles from that staged celebration of the wilderness, manhood, and teamwork, other boys were applying for spots on labor crews—sometimes five applicants vying for one shovel. Those who were hired spent the next decade reshaping the Utah wilderness, one spadeful at a time. They built dams, spread seed, planted trees, established campgrounds, and, on steep mountain slopes like those beneath Shingle Mill Peak, they dug out terraces more than ten feet wide. Inexperienced crewmembers received thirty dollars a month, twenty-five of which was sent home to family, and they were fed and lodged at work camps along the Wasatch Front.

Perhaps on a hot July afternoon that summer, when the last terrace of the day had been dug, and most of the men and boys were heading down the mountain to camp, a few of them put down their shovels and headed for the peak. Perhaps they stepped carefully over the alpine grass and crumbling rock and paused to rest, nostrils full of juniper pollen. Maybe they sat on boulders at the summit and adjusted their socks, pondered the soreness in their backs, and picked at the blisters on their hands. I picture them peering down into the valley, looking for their street, or at least their neighborhood, and I imagine them talking about their families down the mountain, about the children who call them "Papa" and cling to their legs when they come home to visit. Flinging a shovel to bring money home must have felt to them like the most deliberate kind of living—those grown men so full of worry and concern, moving a mountain to make ends meet. But I see the younger boys jostling each other, throwing rocks, and making plans for their time off. Sure they were a cheap labor crew, but the worry of the world may not yet have overtaken them completely. This mountain, to them, may have simply been a mountain, and the only thing essential or deliberate about any of it may have been the way they dared each other to walk to the edge, the way they tossed stones like hand grenades into the void, the way they cupped their palms around their mouths and hollered just to hear their own echoes across the canyon.

"Let us settle ourselves," wrote Thoreau. "And work and wedge our feet downward through the mud and slush of opinion, and prejudice, and tradition, and delusion, and appearance, that alluvion which covers the globe, through Paris and London, through New York and Boston and Concord, through Church and State, through poetry and philosophy and religion, till we come to a hard bottom and rocks in place, which we can call reality."

With a little prodding, the boys rose from their water break, and we began our terrace ascent. But after only a few steps, we heard the sound of that biplane approaching. The noise seemed close, and all of us looked up, but we saw nothing. Leveling my eyes with the mountain saddle, I caught sight of the red, single-engine plane flying right at us. It took a moment to realize that though we were firmly planted on the ground, standing this high on the mountain meant we were very much in the air. The engine noise grew louder, and the boys and I gazed wide-eyed as the pilot, looking through a pair of flight goggles and waving to us from the open cockpit, passed just twenty feet above our heads and then unexpectedly tilted skyward, and began a slow climb. After a few seconds, the plane's engine sputtered and then stalled. For a moment, we stood in perfect silence and stared at the plane suspended above us in the air.

Then the plane rotated downward and twisted in midair like an Olympic platform diver. The engine kicked on again, and the pilot pulled up the nose of the plane and turned away from the mountain and us, heading into the horizon.

The boys whooped and hollered and waved, and for the first time, they seemed genuinely pleased to be up on the mountain. They smiled and shouted and patted each other on the back. We all wished aloud that we'd brought our cameras. Their pace quickened, and for the first time on the trip, I didn't feel like I was dragging them along.

But the optimism lasted only one switchback. Soon they were shuffling their feet again, heads down, seemingly oblivious to the fast-approaching mountaintop. Or weren't they? Perhaps that plane lingered in their minds the way it had lingered in the air. After all, they were out of Gatorade and Pop-Tarts, and the clouds were there to stay, but both boys were still on the trail, one in front of me and one behind me, stepping between root and rock as we approached the summit. None of us could have told you the grand metaphor in that airplane, only that it was small but overwhelming; that its climb was narrow and steep; that its red paint shocked the gray sky; and that watching that plane pivot and float in the air above our heads near the top of that mountain was a kind of personal, if accidental, triumph.

How to Be a T-Ball Parent

Let's suppose that your son is the starting pitcher for his T-ball team. Never mind that he doesn't actually pitch a single ball, and never mind that every one of the players "starts." This is Lubbock, Texas, where Little League is religion, and the jockeying for election starts early.

Like, at six years old.

Your kindergartner had to try out for his T-ball team, and he had to earn that starting spot. On a windy day in late February, you drove him down to the baseball complex on the west side of town and lined him up with sixty other kids in front of a half-dozen clipboard-toting coaches who spent a lot of time furrowing their brows, scratching their chins, and scribbling notes.

Sitting on the bleachers and watching those small boys wait in line, you thought of your own Little League tryouts so many years ago, how it felt to posture for adults, knowing that someone was watching, and how that knowledge made each success somehow sweeter, each failure more frightening. You stood out in the Oregon rain chasing fly balls, each one eaten alive by the cloud-covered sky, until the coach finally called you in because the rain was just too strong. And though the coach reassured you that "no one could catch a ball in that rain," that tight feeling rose in your chest, and you were glad to finally leave. Remember how glad you were it wasn't raining as you watched your own son move forward in line to take his turn at the plate.

You thought then, watching him, that the tryouts were simpler than you'd imagined: step up to the plate and hit three balls, then run around the bases. At third, pick up a glove and field a few grounders, then throw to first. Then move to first and catch for the next boy in line. Hit, run, field, throw, catch, and you're done. At least in theory. Some children could barely hit at all, while others were taking Lou Gehrig cuts that made you whistle. Some kids got a hit and ran down the wrong baseline; others got a hit and just stood there. One small boy bolted from line and refused to get back in it. "I don't know how," he kept saying through tears and a heaving chest. "I don't know how."

But your son did know how. He hit the ball hard, ran hard, and threw hard. He is tall for his age and older than most of the kids out there. He's not the best, but compared to the small boy refusing to get back in line, he might as well be Lou Gehrig. Don't think this, of course, until later when you get to the first practice, and eleven boys and one girl stand on the field, and the coach is trying to run batting practice but instead is chasing a five-year-old named Jerome who's never played a day of baseball in his life and who won't stay at short stop, and three other kids are standing in the outfield with gloves on their heads, and the boy at first base, who is also taller, faster, and stronger than most of the rest of the team, is refusing to retrieve a ball he missed because it rolled under a car parked near the first-base line, and your son is standing at the pitcher's mound pumping his fist into the leather of his glove, knees bent, wondering why the other kids aren't paying more attention. Remember that the former president of Lubbock Little League calls T-ball "the best free family entertainment in town."

You already know this, of course, because before you moved to Texas, your son played T-ball for two years in small-town southeast Ohio where the rules were simple: everyone bats, everyone scores, and everyone wins. Parents came to watch their chubby-legged kindergarteners as they donned Sofa &

Mattress Outlet T-shirts and ran around the infield in a gleeful display of pack behavior that sometimes brought the third baseman, the short stop, and the pitcher out into deep right field chasing a wild grounder. What this kumbaya method lacked in competitive spirit, it more than made up for in congeniality. But you knew then that even if you'd wanted something a little more intense, you would have been out of luck—kumbaya ball was the only gig in town.

So when you moved to Lubbock you were excited. You knew this was a Little League town. You'd seen the well-groomed ball fields dotting the city. You'd heard about the 2007 all-star team that made it all the way to the semifinal round of the Little League World Series, and when you did a little research, you discovered that Lubbock and the surrounding communities are actually divided into seven different Little Leagues, that more than three thousand boys and girls ages four to fourteen fill the rosters of hundreds of teams, that the year is divided into summer and fall ball, and that some teams are "traveling" teams that raise thousands of dollars to compete in tournaments as far away as Cooperstown, New York.

But then at practice you see the coach standing in the middle of the field holding Jerome under one arm as he shouts at the players in the outfield to put on their gloves and tells the boy at first to "Go get the ball!" and you wonder whether or not some of these kids would be better off in the kumbaya league.

Appreciate the coach's patience and his willingness to volunteer. Decide to go stand in the outfield and see what you can do to help. Do this for the first few practices and watch all the kids get used to the idea of a baseball game, the intense focus on the batter, the concerted effort to field the ball and throw it to first base, and then watch one day as Jerome, whose been put in the outfield, realizes none of the balls are going to come to him and so begins chasing down every ball, no matter where it's hit, even pushing over teammates to make the play;

take a deep breath and remind yourself that these are five- and six-year-olds—intensity is definitely relative.

Try not to act surprised when, in addition to the fundamentals of baseball, the coaches teach the players to exploit the loopholes in the T-ball rules. For instance, the rules state that all players must take the field for defense, but do not require coaches to let players try out all the positions. Two boys are all he needs, the coach tells you: pitcher and a first baseman. The slack-jaw kids who can't catch a cold will stay in the outfield the whole season. He doesn't say this, exactly, but that is the impression you get. Your son and the other taller, faster, stronger boy are his ringers. He tells you that most hits by T-ballers never leave the infield, and so every team needs a first baseman who can catch and a pitcher with hot hands and a good arm that can beat the runner to first base. "I think your son is going to be our star," he says.

Listen as the coach tells you about the team that won last year's league championship. "They had this girl who played pitcher." He says, "She was really fast and she ran everyone down. They won every game." Notice again your mild surprise on hearing that T-ball has a league champion. Also recognize for the first time that while the coach is patient and kind, he definitely wants to win, and feel a slight bit of apprehension about how much hope the coach is placing in your son, who at that moment is using his glove as a light saber in a duel with the shortstop. Be glad your son appears to have so much potential, even if the idea of his playing every inning of every game in the most exciting position on the field somehow seems unfair to the other kids.

At the first game, confirm your fear that winning or losing will depend largely on how well your own son plays. Watch him field ball after ball and make clean throws to first. Surprise yourself by shouting, "throw the ball," when one of the smaller players fields it at second base and stands with it over his head. Grimace as the boy with the ball looks around, confused. Wonder if you're feeling empathy or irritation. Grit your teeth when your own son gets confused on the field and runs to the pitcher's mound with the ball because he thinks that's what he needs to do to make the out. Despite yourself, holler something encouraging and gently corrective from the bleachers—something like, "Good hustle, son! Next time throw that ball to first." Glance around after you say this because you know that other parents are watching you. Hope you're not being "*that* dad" and feel reassured when the other parents chuckle. This is, after all, the best free family entertainment in town, and you and your son are both part of the show.

Appreciate the snafus that make the games entertaining, if a little sad. For instance, the five-year-old boy with dead-fish arms who throws the bat every time he swings, which is an automatic out because flying aluminum bats are dangerous. He brings himself to tears, especially after he walks back to the dugout, and his father meets him at the fence and says inaudible words of encouragement or chastisement. Find this sad and funny the first few times, until a late-inning moment one game when the boy refuses to take his turn at the plate because he's absolutely certain he will throw the bat again, that his dead-fish arms will fail him, and that he will have to talk to his dad through the fence one more time.

And consider the center fielder who spends most of every game pulling dandelions from the grass, except for that one particularly windy day when he kept chasing his hat into left field. Or the coach's son, the youngest player on the team, who hits the ball well but whose dachshund legs are no match for the greyhounds in the infield. His run is comical, like Elmer Fudd going the wrong way on an escalator. Remember how the bleachers erupted when he finally made it to first base on a pitcher's throwing error. This boy plays catcher and spends most of his time on defense standing in the shadow of the umpire, raking piles of dirt with his cleats, while out in front of him the game rolls on, and the "pay attention!" mantra of his father echoes in the background.

Then consider your own son, who often gets so caught up in trying to do exactly what he is supposed to do that he forgets to think. Like the day he stands in the batter's box sizing up the ball on the tee and is so startled when the umpire calls "Play ball!" that he turns a check swing into a real swing and trips over his own feet, falling to the ground right in front of the pitcher who picks up the ball and tags him out before he has a chance to stand up. After the game, give your son encouraging advice, tell him that accidents happen, that he'll do better next game, that no one gets on base every time. Tell him about when you were ten and got hit by the batted ball right in the crotch while trying to run from first to second base. Tell him that the umpire called you out for interfering with the play and that you sat in the dugout and cried for the rest of the inning. Don't tell him that the ball hit you more in the pant leg than the crotch, and don't tell him that you played up the injury so people would think your tears were from the pain. Watch your son melt into his own puddle of tears during the ride home and wish to yourself that you hadn't said anything at all.

During the third game of the season, learn a new loophole that your coaches have overlooked. All players must stand in the batter's box before attempting a swing, but there is no rule that says how they must stand in that box. Watch as each opposing batter steps to the plate and then looks toward the third base coach, who directs each batter's feet—"take a step back . . . now turn . . . a little more . . . shift your front foot . . . right there." And then watch each batter respond to the coach like a marionette, lining up his swing with the third baseline. Continue to watch as batter after batter hits the ball toward the third baseman, avoiding your bigger, faster, stronger son almost entirely. He fields some of the balls, but soon the bases are loaded and before you know it, the other team has scored the run limit.

Now your team is batting, and as each player steps to the plate they seem impossibly tiny, and you want your coaches to play marionette with their feet. But they aren't, so you want to say something yourself, but these kids are not your kids and even though you are standing right behind the backstop fence just a few feet from the batters, each of their parents is behind you on the bleachers, and you are not a coach, you are just another dad—the dad of one of the team "stars"—and you worry about what people will think if you start giving unsolicited advice to their kids, so you keep your opinion to yourself, and you watch your son's team hit whoppers to the pitcher who is bigger, faster, and stronger than his teammates and has no trouble fielding the ball and throwing it to first base for the easy out.

Look around at the other parents and wonder to yourself whether they are feeling the same irrational frustration that you are. Think of the advice you heard from the president of one of the other leagues in the next town over—one that plays kumbaya ball and enjoys a reputation for being participation-centric. "Let's put it in perspective," he told you. "These are six-year-old kids playing for an eight-dollar trophy."

Try to put things in perspective.

When you get the chance, call the president of your Little League and ask him about the competitive spirit at T-ball games. Ask him about the funny strategies employed by teams to exploit loopholes in the rules. Ask about the role of competition. Ask about the lopsided scores. Attempt to imply, without saying it, that the system is unfair, that it teaches kids to value winning over learning, and tell him that you're sure some of the kids are just plain bored. Listen as the president of your Little League explains that Lubbock is a baseball town and that the games are competitive because that's what coaches and parents want. Listen as he tells you that people want their kids to have a chance to perform at their best, and that if his league doesn't provide that chance, then those parents will go somewhere else. Avoid asking him what he thinks the players want; avoid asking him whether the kids pulling dandelions in center field are getting a chance to perform at their best. Definitely don't ask if the dandelion puller's $118 fee is buying the same experience as your son's $118.

Of course, you don't need to remind the president of all this, because he has been in Little League for sixteen years, and he has heard all the questions, all the concerns, and he probably shares them. But, in fact, competition is what the parents want—or at least what they think they want. He probably thinks your son is the dandelion puller, or maybe the bat thrower, or maybe the kid who hasn't gotten to first base all season, and so he tells you a story about the first year he coached T-ball, how his team got trounced 25 to 1, how after the handshaking and passing out of snacks, he stood staring at the scoreboard feeling like a failure, when a small boy walked up to him and said, "Hey, Coach, did we win?" The Little League president pauses here for dramatic effect, and you imagine that this is the story he has reserved for parents like you. He says he looked at that kid and asked, "Well, did you have fun?" and when the kid said yes, the sixteen-year veteran of Little League baseball tells you he looked the kid in the eye and said, "then, yeah, you bet we won."

Consider this a fair, if unsatisfying response to your concerns, and then picture the scoreboard at the last game. At the end of four innings, it read 21–7. Most of the game you sat on the bleachers feeling sorry for your son's team—sorry that they hadn't perfected the trick of hitting the ball down the third-base line, sorry that the other team seemed so capable in the infield, sorry that your son's team wasn't bigger, faster, and stronger. Then think about your son who climbed into the car after the game with a juice box in his hand and a package of fruit snacks. Remember the way he smiled and said, "Hey, Dad, did you see the scoreboard? We got seven runs!" And hold that image in your mind—tell yourself that this is what it's all about, that the Little League president is right when he says the scoreboard is for the parents and the coaches, and feel a little silly for getting so wrapped up in your son's game, and then, as you put the car in gear to leave, promise yourself that you'll teach him that third-base trick before his next one.

The Swing Is Gone

A dancer's body is a work of art—all pose and proportion, angle and frame, tone and balance, texture and taut muscle. Men built like Roman sculptures, women built like, well, dancers—everything long, thin, and controlled, like floating silk, poured sand, spiraled steel. The communion of beat and step, the study of jump and glide, the celebration of move and stop—*that* is dance.

But that is not what we, the forty or so Introduction to Dance students staring at ourselves in the mirrors of the studio, were even remotely close to imagining. We were thinking about feet: about keeping them off each other; moving forward, back, one-two-three; back, forward, one-two-three. Left foot for men, right for women. And we were thinking about our hands—lower than waltz, higher than swing. Bodies close. Feet tied in knots. Forward, back, one-two-three; back, forward, one-two-three.

Don't worry about your hips, the instructor kept saying—the woman with the hips that rolled like a bolt of satin unspooling. Don't worry about your hips. But this is Latin dance—the cha-cha—so I must worry about my hips. All I can think about are my hips, her hips. How does she do that?

It happened during a water break. My wife, Melissa, was at the drinking fountain or in the bathroom, and there I was, staring at the mirror, thinking about my hips. Forward, back, one-two-three; back, forward, one-two-three. Learning Latin hips is like learning to ride a bike—once you get it, the roll of your hips feels natural; until you get it, you look like a man with a squirrel down his shorts. I hadn't gotten it. The instructor with the satin hips turned her head in my direction and caught me squirreling in the mirror.

Then she was laughing. Forward, back, one-two-three. Red-faced and crying. Back, forward, one-two-three. He's trying to free a wedgie, she must be thinking. Forward, back, one-two-three. I'm sorry, she mouthed when our eyes met, and she turned away.

But it was not her fault, this laughing—no. It was that natural, insuppressible laugh beautiful women reserve for men who step on rakes, who catch Frisbees in the crotch, who lose their toupees in the soup.

Once upon a time, I thought I might be like that woman with the hips. A dancer. Make movement my life, rhythm my time clock. Back then I danced for the gasp of the gawking crowds, for my arms around a pretty girl, for the rush of music keeping time with body. Dance could have been my road less traveled, the dream I chose to chase. I don't think about it very often anymore, except when a certain song comes on the radio, and the drums and the brass and the strings tap into a part of me I've forgotten, perhaps buried, and I wonder how I became that guy the pretty dance instructor laughed at.

I learned to dance from an eleven-year-old girl named Leslie. She was new in our school and awkward in her long, brown ponytail and flowered dress. It was on the bus, I think, that she asked me to be her dance partner for a school talent show. I didn't know jazz, and I'd never heard of swing. What did I know? I knew what my girls-have-cooties friends would think, and so I wanted to say no, meant to say no, opened my mouth to say no, but something—perhaps the chance to be on stage, perhaps the shimmer of Leslie's brown hair—stopped me, and what came out was, "Sure."

Every day after school for several weeks, we practiced in her sunroom. She had the music, the routine, and even her dress picked out. In the background somewhere, I remember her mother nodding approvingly but not coaching. Leslie taught me everything. She placed my right hand on her side and held my left hand high with hers: my first "dance position." I don't remember footwork, or counting, or even that my movements were supposed to work in concert with the music coming from the small tape deck sitting in the corner of the room. She coaxed me through the steps, teaching me where to put my feet, where to turn and place my hands, but mostly she wanted me to get out of the way so she could spin.

Onstage the day of the show, in front of the entire school, wearing slacks and a necktie my mother helped me loop, I held Leslie's hand as the music played and she twisted in her iridescent green dress. And when the music picked up, and she twirled under my arm, and the dress spun like fireworks exploding, I remember the noise the crowd made, and I remember whispering, "That got 'em." And I wondered if they'd gasped because of the twirl or because her dress had come up too high, and I felt that moment like a metaphor. I had no idea what I was doing, but I liked it. I didn't care what my friends in the crowd would (and did) say to me afterward. I was on stage. With a girl. And the crowd was breathless.

By middle school, my cootie-phobic friends had decided girls weren't such a bad idea, and we went schizophrenic trying out different kinds of music, different kinds of dance, looking for ways to get those girls into our arms.

In sixth grade, we tried sagging our pants on suburban streets and watching the parents of our rougher friends drink malt liquor from tall bottles that said St. Ides and Olde English. We listened to Snoop Dogg and Dr. Dre on a pair of second-hand speakers and tried to look cool for the blonde girl next door. We sipped Mountain Dew at tweenage house parties with Boyz II Men on the stereo and stayed out way past dark. Dance of choice: freak. Willing partner: a tall girl named Anna who taught me how to on a dare and then giggled through the entire gyratory fiasco.

By seventh grade, we'd moved on to Seattle grunge. Friends crammed into my living room for my thirteenth birthday wearing thermal tops under Green Day T-shirts. Nirvana's *Nevermind* boomed on a set of stage speakers perched on my mom's sewing table. Airwalks and Doc Martens tapped the floor; heads banged. People clapped me on the back and said, "Sweet party, dude!" Dance of choice: mosh pit. We'd exchanged slow-jam hip thrusts for full-body contact in a shy, ironic, slam-into-you-as-hard-as-I-can-because-I-like-you sort of way. Willing partners: forty friends from school—at least until my mom caught my friend Tim stage-diving off the back of the couch, and another friend split his forehead open on someone's tooth.

I blame a drama class for what happened at the eighth-grade cafeteria talent show: me and three friends in white T-shirts and jeans, like the Fonz, and "Earth Angel," by the Penguins, playing on the loudspeaker. A captive audience of peers on their lunch hour watched as we snapped our fingers, stepped in time, and Marty, our baby-faced lead singer, jumped off the stage to lip-sync the bridge. Girls in the audience screamed. Actually screamed. Dance of choice: snapping fingers and making eyes at girls through dark sunglasses. Willing partner: Who cares! I was snapping my fingers on stage in a pair of sunglasses.

Somewhere between high-school hangouts and church dances, I rediscovered the big-band jazz and the swing dancing Leslie had introduced me to in elementary school. And I also discovered the aerial lift. I didn't know the difference between East Coast Swing and West Coast Swing, the triple step, or the Lindy Hop, but I knew that with the right partner and a little practice, I could pull off lifts with names like the candlestick, around-the-world, shoot-the-gap, and rag-doll. And to that end, I practiced—a lot.

I rehearsed steps every Saturday at church dances with any girl who would hang on tight; I practiced at my high school with kids from the swing-dance club, in my friend's basement, and in my living room. I watched the movie *Swing Kids* like it was a workout video. I bought a fedora and wore it with wingtips and suspenders, carried a crook-handled umbrella to dances, and bought a slew of CDs with titles like *The Big Band Collection*, *Glen Miller's Greatest Hits*, and *Swing Time*. I learned famous songs like "Sing, Sing, Sing," "Tuxedo Junction," and "It Don't Mean a Thing If It Ain't Got That Swing," and the not-so-famous songs—ballads like "Tangerine," drum-thumping dance tunes like "Big Noise from Winnetka," and even a song called "Happiness Is a Thing Called Joe," a slow croon I listened to over and over, imagining myself as someone's definition of happiness. I dated a girl whose parents let us clear the furniture out of their living room, and we danced in our socks to Duke Ellington, Count Basie, Brian Setzer, Cherry Poppin' Daddies, and Squirrel Nut Zippers. Swing did everything dance was supposed to do—it got a girl in my arms, it got a crowd cheering, and it put me in touch with a wild part of myself: a flamboyant, unruly, artsy part of myself that couldn't get enough.

I found a dance club on Portland's east side, set up in an old Masonic temple. A few times a month, a ten-piece orchestra played a set. Five bucks got you in, and you could dance until midnight. Hot lights, warm oak, cool dancing. The men wore spats and vests, and the women wore shorts under their skirts.

The first time I went, I thought I would be wowed by the acrobatics and learn some new ways to make the crowds cheer, but this club was not about lifts. It was about footwork: dynamite, whirlwind footwork; playful, flirty, seductive footwork. Rockstep-triplestep-backstep-stomp. Roundstep-triplestep-backstep-kick.

I finally learned the difference between the triple step and the Lindy Hop—learned moves like the sugar foot, the Charleston, and the octopus. This club was school. Boot camp. A monastery. Home.

Except it wasn't. I didn't go to the club nearly as often as I could have. Didn't have the guts to ask a stranger there, one of the women who really knew how to dance, to show me around the floor; never got beyond the moves I picked up in church dance groups or pulled out of dance scenes from movies or saw others do at the club. I felt young. Out of my league. Timid. And the truth I kept buried somewhere was this: I didn't love to dance. Not as much as I told myself I did. If I had, I would have joined a team, hired a teacher, and gotten serious. At least, that's how I felt. The dancing had earned me a bit of social capital—girls liked that I could dance, and I liked that I could dance, and I really liked that girls liked that I could dance. But in that club, I came up against an unpleasant truth about the difference between talent and skill. Dance was going to take some real commitment, and it had to be about more than crowds and girls.

Still, the few formal instructors I worked with on occasion all said I should seriously consider dancing for real. "You can go to college on your dancing," one woman said. And walking out of the club in Portland one of those first nights when I'd stared in disbelief at the kick and stomp and play on the dance floor and had tried in a clumsy, imitative way to re-create the moves I'd seen, a stranger tapped me on the shoulder and said, "Hey, nice work out there. You can really feel the music."

After graduating from high school, I moved to Japan to serve as an LDS missionary. For two years, I traded in a dance partner and any decision about my future in dance for a mission companion and twelve hours a day of knocking on doors, talking to people on the street, and teaching free English-conversation classes. No time for dancing, and little thought of girls. But then I moved to Tokushima, a city of rivers and bridges on the east coast of Shikoku Island, which plays host to Japan's largest dance festival, the Awa Odori.

The day I arrived in Tokushima, folk music greeted me over the PA system at the train station. Photographs of dancers in traditional garb hung from the walls, and everywhere outside the station were sculptures of traditional-looking folk dancers in wry poses. I had arrived two weeks before the late-summer festival, but even if it had been the middle of winter, I would have seen dance in the arched bridges poised over the quiet water, heard it in the traffic that bobbed and weaved around the mountains, and felt it in the ocean breeze rolling in from the east. Tokushima trembled with dance and hummed with the bygone sound of drums.

The Awa Odori is not a couple's dance. Instead, men and women parade through the streets in separate groups, performing very different steps. The women dance in light kimonos called *yukatas* and hold their hands in the air, curved gently at the wrists, bodies leaning forward on their *geta* sandals. They advance with small steps and kick their legs back, turning their bodies side to side ever so slightly, like vertical blinds flickering open and closed.

The men wear *happi* coats, white cotton shorts, and white, split-toe socks called *tabi*. They wear bandanas tied around their foreheads, and when they dance, they squat low and take short, deliberate steps while waving paper fans in both hands, cutting triangles in the air.

Both men and women dance to the same *taiko* drum rhythms accompanied by small *kane* bells and *shamisens*—long stringed instruments worn like guitars and plucked with wooden picks called *bachi*. For more than fifty years, musicians and dancers have gathered on the streets of Tokushima in mid-August, and more than a million people come to the city every year to watch.

At church, I asked a young man if he was going.

"Going?" he repeated, striking a pose I recognized from posters in the train station. "I'm performing." He said we should come watch, and he introduced us to his parents. "I bet they'd show you around."

Their names were Miyako and Kenji Tanaka, and they had met more than forty years earlier while dancing the Awa Odori. The night of the festival, we rode our bicycles to their home. On their wall hung an old municipal poster of the two of them dancing side by side but separate, each one poised and concentrating—her hands in the air, his out in front of him. "We didn't know each other then," she said to me, pointing at the poster. The Tanakas met while dancing the Awa Odori and have been dancing together for decades.

Mr. Tanaka drove us all to the festival in his car—a Toyota Crown Wagon with white lace stretched across the backs of the seats. He dropped us off near the entrance to the festival and waved good-bye. We would spend the next few hours wandering through the crowds, admiring the costumes, tasting the food, absorbing the music, and maybe even joining in on the parade. I couldn't understand why Mr. Tanaka, with all his history of dance, wouldn't want to join us.

"He's not staying?" I asked Mrs. Tanaka as she led us into the crowd.

"Mr. Tanaka does not like to watch," she said over her shoulder. "Now that he's too old to dance."

I came home from Japan eager to pursue dance in college, eager to travel the country as part of a team, maybe even travel the world. Perhaps I'd even marry a dancer. It all seemed such an irresistibly romantic notion—the way dance could hold a couple together: such an easy metaphor, such an easy date idea.

My first year of college at Brigham Young University, I gave it a try. BYU has the largest dance program in the country, and the entry-level social dance classes were a gateway to if not fame and fortune, then at least a college career as an amateur dancer. If you wanted to make it onto one of BYU's award-winning teams, you had to start at the intro level. That semester, all beginning ballroom classes were full, so I signed up for western social dance, where I learned the two-step.

For men, the Texas two-step is all about the buckle—the cowboy badge of cool, a place to rest one's hand when it's not holding onto one's partner, a steering wheel, a pivot point, a pole around which the cowboy turns. The buckle and the boots, and the heeling and toeing and swinging like a man slouched at a bar, resembled everything I loved about swing, but it had a lazy locomotion, both casual and proper—a dance version of southern hospitality.

Right about this time, I began dating a girl named Melissa. She was tall, with dark hair and a cautious smile, and she had a thing for modern architecture and strawberry Life Savers. We'd started dating in Portland before coming to Utah for school, and one of the first things I wanted to know about her was whether or not she danced. Did her toes tap in the car? Did she twirl in the kitchen to the radio? Had she ever sweat through her shirt on a dance floor? I played country music on the radio when I picked her up for a first date to gauge her reaction, and on our third date, I took her down to that old Masonic Temple dance hall for a baptism by fire.

That was my first time back to the dance hall in years, and I was surprised to see the orchestra replaced by a CD player. In the two years I had been gone, the floors had been neglected, and the lighting had somehow lost its charm. And when I took Melissa by the hand and walked her out to the middle of the floor, it didn't take long for me to realize that she was in unfamiliar territory. She followed me around the floor the whole night, rock-stepping and ball-changing her way through a crash course in the four-step swing, the Charleston, and a simplified imitation of the Lindy Hop that I'd picked up in high school. We weren't the graceful work of art I'd hoped for—not much to look at with our knee-knocking and toe-mashing and aerial lifts that only narrowly avoided crash landings. But if she hadn't been blessed with the rhythm and coordination I was looking for, she had been blessed with the courage to keep trying. She never asked to sit out, never clammed up, and at the end of the night, we'd both sweat through our shirts.

My own self-consciousness about our awkward performance should have left me shamed, should have been cause enough to drop Melissa off early, to cut my losses and tell her I'd see her around. But that's not what happened. I wouldn't say I'd fallen in love—that would be too neat and tidy. No, I wasn't in love, yet, but there was something to Melissa and the way she spun and stepped and laughed at herself and kept trying, and I was intrigued.

As part of my Western Social Dance course, I had to compete in the BYU Dancesport Championship's amateur two-step competition. My partner was a tall, freckle-faced girl named Rhonda, who had a red ponytail and a natural affinity for Wranglers, and leading up to the competition, we spent several hours a week practicing in a spare room on campus. By then, Melissa and I were in the spend-every-waking-moment-together stage of our relationship, and so while I spent all my dance time with Rhonda, I did all my other competition prep with Melissa. She helped me pick out the black Wranglers and the pin-striped western shirt with mother-of-pearl snaps I'd wear during the competition. She went with me to a costume store to rent a cowboy hat, and she even helped me track down a large, gold buckle as a finishing touch to the whole outfit.

Rhonda and I made it all the way to the final round, and Melissa was there to cheer us on. She took our picture holding our second-place trophy, and she walked me home at the end of the night. As we walked, I imagined what it might be like a few years down this Dancesport road. If things went well with dance and with Melissa, this would be only the first of many evenings for her standing on the sidelines, and though she seemed supportive, I wasn't sure I could handle a hobby that made the woman in my life feel like a third wheel. Of course, that's the life of a dancer. A partner is a partner, and it's just business—the time you spend in the arms of another woman is just a sacrifice you're willing to make if dancing is your dream. And that sacrifice, I realized then, was the problem—and, ultimately, the solution to the question I'd been struggling to answer for months.

After I finished the class, I decided to put the idea of competitive dance on the shelf for a while. Instead I put my energy into teaching Melissa the two-step, while we tried to figure out whether we should really spend the rest of our lives together. We found a community center in the next town over that held country dances on the weekends, and we spent a lot of time struggling through footwork, timing, and turns. But off the floor we were stealing the show. We'd actually arrived at that romantic-comedy-montage stage—the two of us throwing our heads back in laughter as we cooked a cheap meal together in her small apartment, the two of us taking a long evening walk as the moon rose behind us, the two of us holding hands in a darkened theater, stealing kisses during class, exchanging gifts, sharing lunches, and, yes, occasionally stepping on each other's toes on the dance floor.

That was March. We were married in August.

Growing up, it seemed like opportunities were constantly expanding. I could be and do anything. Freedom was my greatest ally, time my greatest asset, and imagination my only boundary. But the gravitational pull of adulthood set in motion what felt at first like a slow contraction. College meant independence, but it also meant choosing a path in life. And marriage meant companionship, but it also meant compromise. Melissa and I went dancing every once in a while but not enough to keep up what I'd learned, and by the time we took that social dance class where the instructor with the satin hips caught me contorting in the mirror, I'd officially crossed the line to that place where dancing was something I used to do.

A few years into our marriage, Melissa and I took our two-year-old son to Tokushima for the Awa Odori festival. I told them of the city, the music, and the dancing. I told them about the Tanakas, the old couple who had introduced me to the festival, about how they'd met and about their years of dance.

But when we met the Tanakas at their door, I could tell something had changed. Mr. Tanaka, who was old when I met him the first time, was now in the advanced stages of multiple sclerosis. He couldn't walk up his own stairs. He couldn't even drive us to the festival. We left him sitting on the floor of his living room, watching television and, slowly, with trembling hands, pulling the skin off a cold, purple grape.

Mrs. Tanaka took us to the festival. She explained the difference between the bird dance and the kite dance, and the men's and women's dances, too. She showed us how to step in line and wave our hands in triangles. We found a seat and watched the parade of dancers come by. They were singing, and I asked Mrs. Tanaka what the words meant.

"You're a fool if you dance," she said, smiling. "And you're a fool if you don't." She smiled wider. "So if you're going to be a fool, you might as well dance."

Shortly after that, her son came down the street with his group, and he danced toward us, stepping lightly on the asphalt. He waved his fans playfully in my son's face, smiled at him, and tried to coax him out into the street to step with the beat of the *taiko* drums. Instead, my son buried his head in my shirt, afraid, perhaps, of how the dance might move him.

Melissa and I still talk about going dancing. We survived the intro class and still remember a bit of the cha-cha, even if I can't do the hips, and we tell ourselves we'd dance more if there were a place nearby, if there were time. But we juggle kids now, and I teach college, and we've got responsibilities at church, and there's always a jelly sandwich flipped upside down on the carpet to worry about, and a movie is easier and cheaper and less involved than finding a dance hall.

It would be easy to lay the blame on her, but the truth is, I think the noise would be daunting to me, the crowds too unwieldy. I haven't sweat through a dress shirt in years; I can't remember the last time I opened a circle on a crowded dance floor with little more than a few spins of my partner, lifting her over my head and then twirling her in an arc across the floor, watching the wake of her skirt tails rippling behind her. And given the chance, I don't think I could anymore. I'm not old—barely thirty—but something's gone. Time? Desire? A partner? Something else. My wife and I do dance, but it's different. There's no show involved. No crowd. No adolescent hubris, no chase. Instead, we turn around our kitchen the way I imagine lovers are supposed to—I curl her under my arm and dip her slowly, dramatically, and kiss her in a comfortable, familiar way. And when I do, my stomach still flips the way it did the first time I kissed her, but we live at waltz speed now, and a part of me is sad the swing is gone.

Still, on the occasional Saturday morning, while flipping pancakes on the griddle for my boys, I put on Ellington or Basie or Miller and hear the roll of drums and the hum of clarinets and trumpets and the thump-twang of bass strings, and I imagine that I never turned away from dancing, that I didn't quit before enthusiasm could become real talent. And if no one's around, and I've got the space, I lay down a few counts of the Charleston, one foot in front of the other, and then back, an ankle-twisting question mark of a dance step. Am I coming or going? Bowing out or cutting in? Calling it a night, or just getting started?

On Haptics, Hyperrealism, and
My Father's Year in Prison

Beneath the thin cotton layer of my wife's shirt, beneath the stretch of skin and muscle, a small fetal body rolled and flinched. I watched the tectonic shifts of her belly and then placed my hand against her abdomen to feel the distinct press of a small foot pushing back against my palm. Melissa had grown accustomed to all the movement, but to me, the pressure of this heel on my palm was novel—a fresh sign that the bump of her belly contained, not some romantic notion or hypothetical possibility, but an actual child, a little person that together we'd called into being.

Of the five senses, touch is the first to develop. With it, we explore the narrow confines of the womb; we discover the first inklings of what it means to draw a line between the who of our body and the what of the space around us. And after nine months of exploring the walls of that cave, we are born into the light, limbs groping, eyes searching, little digits and receptors thirsty for more.

For each of their first few months of life, it seemed that my boys experienced the world as one long nap, interrupted only by the need to nurse or defecate, and sometimes they managed to sleep even through that. At a few weeks old, my youngest son, Ian, fit squarely in the crook of my arm and rode along as I picked up his older brothers' toys in the living room, or pulled a snack from the refrigerator, or typed one-handed at the keyboard. He sometimes roused himself long enough to look about, to flick or flail an arm, but mostly he just slept, limp-limbed and leaning against my chest. At the top of his head, beneath a thin veil of hair, was his soft spot, slowly pulsing with his heartbeat, a location of such immediate vulnerability that I found it difficult to look at and impossible to touch.

Haptic memory is the memory of touch, the split-second recall of immediate tactile stimuli, and without it, human beings would struggle to navigate the physical world. We would have difficulty judging weight and density; it would be nearly impossible to type on a keyboard, open a bottle, chop vegetables, or shave. However, of all our memory systems, haptic memory is the most fleeting, and in order to remember touch over the long term, we must attach it to the other physical and emotional memories. Touch may be responsible for our first encounters with the world, but alone it will never be enough to keep us connected.

The night my father told me he might go to prison, he sat me down in our living room on the couch, put an arm around me, and explained the situation—something about trouble at work, a crooked boss, an inept lawyer, no money for appeal, and the distinct possibility that he would have to go away for a year. I was eight, the youngest, and the last of my brothers and sisters to know. Dad would be appearing in court the next day, and he could no longer put off telling me. I don't remember the words he said, nor was I old enough to empathize with the guilt and shame he must have been feeling. But I do remember how his wool sweater itched my face, how I didn't mind the scratch of his five o'clock shadow when he hugged me, how the loose threads in the floral pattern of the couch poked up at my palm, and how after he'd gone away, I would sit out on that couch alone and run my fingers over the bumps and curves of the stitching.

On most nights, I walk through my front door and two-year-old Ian tackles me in the entryway. He and his five-year-old brother, Nolan, chant "Daddy, Daddy" as they hop in a circle around me. Ian grabs my leg and says "hold you," while Nolan pulls on my hand and asks me to pick him up. I have been gone years if I have been gone hours, and when I come back home, they want piggyback rides, and they want to wrestle, and they want to squeeze me until I can't breathe. And mostly, I think they want contact—skin and muscle and pressure—they want to bounce their energy off something; they want, I imagine, some tactile proof that they're alive, that they're not alone, and that when they reach out, someone will reach back.

In Pennsylvania a few years ago, a ninety-one-year-old woman named Jean Stevens made headlines when the police discovered she'd been living with the embalmed corpses of her husband, who'd been gone for a decade, and her sister, who had only recently been buried in Jean's backyard. Her husband had a place in the garage on an old sofa, where his body sat propped up for conversation, and her sister got a daybed in a room across the hall from Jean's. When a reporter asked the old woman why she'd had her husband and sister exhumed, Jean answered, "I think when you put them in the [ground], that's good-bye, good-bye. In this way I could touch her and look at her and talk to her."

Ron Mueck is a hyperrealist sculptor who molds awkward, self-conscious people out of silicone, polyester resin, and synthetic hair. His nude and nearly nude sculptures of men, women, and children look so real that you almost expect them to move, to shift in their seats, to turn their heads and say, "What are you looking at?" And even when Mueck works on an exaggerated scale, creating, say, a fifteen-foot-tall little boy squatting in the corner or a newborn baby the size of a pickup truck, our minds play tricks, and we succumb to what critic Susan Greeves calls "the overwhelming desire to touch." His bodies should evoke corpses in their stillness, but instead, I feel as if I'm peeking in someone's window. I can't help imagining movement in the wrinkled nose of a baby, breath in the parted lips of a laboring woman, voice in the throat of the little boy who stands in his underwear—his neck bent forward, his arms straight, and his hands curled self-consciously behind his back. Mueck's people are practically bursting with story, as if each is carrying a secret and is just waiting for the right hand to light on its shoulder.

The morning of my father's final court appearance, I sat with the rest of my family on a long wooden bench outside the courtroom, waiting for the verdict. We'd all come to watch—my mother, my two older brothers, my sister, and the baby—each of us an integral part of the defense lawyer's appeal for mercy. Instead, we were ushered out of the room so we wouldn't have to hear the witnesses speak ill of our father. We sat on the benches and waited, huddled together like some scene from a Dickens novel, and when the guilty verdict came down, and my father came out of the courtroom, we hugged him and then said good-bye and watched him walk away down the marbled hallway, his shoulders stooped, his wrists pulled behind him by the handcuffs, his hands somehow boyish in the way they curled and hung limp at his back, drawn so close but not quite touching.

My oldest son, Callan, no longer greets me at the door as he used to. Often while his younger brothers are whirling around the room, drunk on my mere presence, he remains on the couch, his nose in a book, apparently oblivious to my arrival. He looks up when I say hello and still occasionally comes over for a hug, but more and more, he's aloof—not with the oedipal disdain of a teenager but with a casualness that comes, I think, from a growing confidence that he can stand alone on the spinning world without the fear of falling over.

For the longest time AT&T's marketing slogan was "reach out and touch someone"—an ingenious campaign that made the telephone a part of us: a shoulder to lean on, a long distance hug, a wire-to-wire kiss on the cheek.

The first time I spoke with my father after watching bailiffs escort him down the hall at the courthouse, we talked through the receiver of a wall-mounted telephone in the visiting area of a low-security prison outside Portland, Oregon. He wore an orange jump suit and sat on one side of a glass partition while Mom and five kids sat on the other. We took turns at the phone, but I don't remember anything he said, only that his voice sounded distant and slightly mechanical and that the crowding on our side of the glass seemed as comical as the solitude on his side of the glass seemed miserable. We fidgeted and fought for space near Mom and elbowed our way forward to see Dad and grimaced at the scrubbed austerity of the prison's heavy doors and parade of stern faces. We didn't stay long, and we never came back, except Mom, who went nearly every week for six months by herself, because taking the kids was just too hard she told me. She doesn't remember ever missing a visit, but she must have because she does remember sitting down at that glass partition one week and picking up the phone and hearing my father say, "You didn't come."

A body wants to be touched. It's in our DNA. And even slight momentary contact can affect us more than we probably realize. If your waiter touches you on the shoulder or arm while taking your order, you're more likely to buy extra drinks and leave a better tip. If the librarian touches your hand as he passes back your library card, you're more likely to think he's a nice person. Bus drivers are more likely to give you a free ride if you touch them on the shoulder when you ask for one. Strangers who share a conversation while holding hands are more likely to find one another attractive. In medical care, therapeutic touch can slow a heart rate, decrease blood pressure, and reduce anxiety. The well-placed hand of a caregiver can reduce a dying patient's sense of isolation, can even muffle the dread of imminent death.

Before spending a decade as a corpse propped up in his own garage, James Stevens had been Jean's husband of more than sixty years. They were high school sweethearts before he went off to fight in the war, and after he returned, he worked for General Electric and then as a mechanic for most of their married life before passing away from Parkinson's disease in 1999. When reporters from the AP visited Jean's home, they took a photo of the widow out in her yard holding a framed black-and-white photograph of her and her husband. In the old photo, a young Jean looks directly into the camera, while a young James stands just behind her, leaning in ever so slightly, as if propping her up. But the ninety-one-year-old Jean holding that frame stands alone in her backyard, and the young couple in the photo seems to lean against her, as if the wrinkled hands that cradle them are the only things keeping them together.

Our existence depends upon our sense of touch. Without it, writes the philosopher Michel Serres, "There would be no internal self, no body properly speaking; we would live without consciousness; slippery smooth and on the point of fading away."

After six months in the low-security prison, my father graduated to the Rajneesh Hotel, a state-run halfway home from which he and the other inmates could leave each morning for work and return each night by curfew. More like a youth hostel than a penitentiary, the hotel featured a fitness room, an open lobby with comfortable chairs, and a small cafeteria with a few rows of tables, a coffeemaker, and a juice dispenser—all selling points for my mother, who decided she could once again manage bringing us kids with her on her weekly visits. We went several times in that half year, but it's our first visit that sticks out most in my mind.

Dad met us in the foyer. He was all laughs and hugs and stories about the other inmates as he gave us a tour of the public area and showed us the new holes he had punched in his belt because he'd lost so much weight using the fitness room. In that moment I had little capacity to read my father's behavior, to recognize the sense of apology in his voice, the way he kept hugging us, reassuring us that he was glad for our visit, glad to be in the Rajneesh, glad to be a step closer to home. He let me hang from his flexed bicep and told us all over again how great he felt. And when he turned to me and patted his taut stomach and told me to punch him, I had the vague notion that he was showing off, that he needed us to see that he was still Dad, still the man, a rock, untouchable.

Jean Stevens had always been close to her sister, June, but after James died, they grew even closer. They talked on the phone several times a week and wrote letters across the 200 miles that separated them. But in 2009, when doctors told June she had cancer, phone calls and letters were no longer enough. Death, I believe, shines the brightest light on our loneliest corners, and it's not difficult to imagine what was going through Jean's mind when she went to Connecticut to be with her sister. Not difficult to imagine why they shared a bed, why Jean rubbed her sister's back while June tried to sleep through the pain. And in that light, it's not quite as difficult to imagine why, after June had died, Jean would ask neighbors to dig up her sister's body, why she would prop up that body in a spare bedroom across the hall, why she would do her sister's makeup, dress her in a house coat, and spritz her with expensive perfume. Jean knew her story would sound odd, even creepy, to many people, and she knew some would make light of it—even pointed out to a journalist that Jay Leno had made a joke about her—but as I read more of her story, it's not the macabre details I keep coming back to, but Jean's desire to keep her sister alive. "I'd go in," she told the AP reporter, "and I'd talk, and I'd forget."

Before you and I could speak, we used touch, among other nonverbal methods, to make ourselves heard. And some scientists believe that when you and I revert to a preverbal approach to getting our point across, we are simply backsliding down the line of our "evolutionary heritage." For proof, spend an afternoon with my three boys when they've missed a nap or their snack time, and they're struggling under the burden of a toy-distribution inequity, or couch-cushion real-estate scarcity, or some other small-child turmoil, and watch as my living room devolves into a teeth-gnashing, chest-thumping, ground-pounding, chasing, hitting melee to rival any troop of chimpanzees careening through a jungle. But what if turning to physicality—to our bodies, to our hands—is not always a sign of regression? What if sometimes we're at our most humane, our most evolved, when we shut our mouths and open our arms?

I read books with my boys every night. I make up stories and sing lullabies. I rub Callan's back, wrap up Nolan in his blanket, and rock with Ian in the chair until he rubs his eyes and yawns and points to his toddler-sized mattress on the floor. These nights are sweet-memories-in-the-making and help convince me I'm a halfway decent father. But some nights I'm tired, and the house is a mess, and I'm distracted by some work I've brought home, and the boys are pulling each other's ears, and I lose it. On a recent night like this, I found myself yelling at Nolan for some forgettable five-year-old infraction, and as he stood there cowering before my unreasonable expectations, I could see myself yelling, could hear the absurdity of my own frustrated voice, and could see, for once, how I must have looked to him: large, frightening, and impossible to please—utterly untouchable in my anger. I was just another meaty animal, capable of little more than beating my chest and dragging my son through the underbrush.

By the time I stopped myself and left the room, the damage was already done. My son stood by himself, hyperventilating from shame, fear, and frustration, and I felt small, lifeless, and alone, totally exposed and completely at his mercy. Nothing I could say or do would make it right in that moment, but I couldn't do nothing, so I went back in the room, knelt on the floor beside my son, and hugged him, convinced again that a father's only hope is to treat his boys in such a way that when they grow old enough to hear it, they will accept the apology he most certainly owes them.

In a rare self-portrait sculpture titled *Mask* (2001), Ron Mueck offers viewers just the surface of his scowling face, from the top of his creased forehead to the bottom of his wrinkled chin. The sculpture, almost five feet tall, more than four feet wide, and hung from wires attached to the ceiling so that it floats disembodied in the air, is the artist's attempt to re-create his own angry face as seen from his young daughter's perspective. The high-precision detail, from the stubble growing on his chin to the subtle crow's-feet around his eyes to the pockmark on the tip of his nose, effectively puts the artist under a microscope. And the slight embellishment of the features, from the sharpened, terse lips that might be about to spit to the furrowed eyebrows jutting downward in an angry, exaggerated V, suggests that while this is an angry face, it is also a comic one—tragically comic. In lampooning himself at his worst, Mueck appears to understand that there is something silly and embarrassing about an adult who lets a child get to him. And in disembodying himself, he seems to recognize the way our own anger can put the world out of reach.

The subject of my father's arrest and subsequent yearlong incarceration is a touchy one for my family. We're all grown up now, but my brothers and sisters almost never talk about it, and even bringing it up the few times I did in order to fill in details for this retelling made for some awkward conversations. Admittedly, I was young when it all happened and could not feel, as my older brothers and sisters felt, and certainly as my mother felt, the full emotional toll of having Dad in jail for a year. It was real for them in a way it will never be real for me, and so I worry a little about telling their story. The experience for me is largely wrapped in snippets of memory I can only halfway parse, and even though I am convinced this story can explain much of what I do and how I feel as a father today, I still find myself guessing, extrapolating, imagining, and groping for some metaphor, some external way of making this more than just a sad story of what it was like as a child to witness my father's biggest failure before I knew what failure was.

No charges were ever brought against Jean Stevens for disinterring her husband and her twin sister, but the coroner did insist on confiscating the bodies until she built a mausoleum to hold them. And build she did, a shed-cum-crypt right on her property, large enough to hold as many as eight bodies and close enough for Jean to visit the pair every day, to sit beside them and peer in at their faces through the clear panels on their body bags. It was likely her husband's family that originally alerted the authorities to Jean's situation, concerned, I imagine, about the unearthed corpses they felt ought to remain buried. On the one hand, I can see the closure of burial, of leaving a person to memory, of letting a story rest, but on the other hand, I can see Jean's desire to keep them above ground, to revisit them, hoping, perhaps, that the story might find a way to rewrite itself.

The difference between a touching story and one that manipulates us is, of course, a question of force. All of us want to feel moved, but no one wants to be manhandled.

My father only spent a year in prison, and it was more than twenty years ago. That time neither defines him, nor does it define our relationship, and yet I keep coming back to it—this most poignant of reminders that my father was less than perfect, less than the mythic being most boys see when they see their fathers—and even though I know it's unfair to dwell on it, I do. And perhaps it's not about him at all but about me and my own boys and what they might recall twenty years from now as they review the laundry list of pedestrian transgressions that will, over the years, render me mortal before them, reveal me in flesh and blood, leave me naked and bare, without a mask to hide behind. I am well acquainted with the fear, anger, and frustration a father can stir in his son, but before I had my own boys, I thought such emotions were a one-way street. And now, as I imagine them looking back on their boyhoods, I have the sudden desire to put my arm around my father and hold him until he accepts the apology I've begun to think that I might owe him.

Ron Mueck's rendition of his father stands out among his other work for one striking reason—the sculpture is of his father's corpse. In nearly every other sculpture, Mueck takes great pains to convince us that his subjects are alive, that if we look away they might blink, sit up, or lean over and tap us on the shoulder. However, the withered eyes, sunken mouth, limp limbs, and naked, prone posture of *Dead Dad* (1996) point definitively to the inevitable final chapter of mortality. But more than that, they point to a relationship between father and son that is as sad as it is unknowable. The sculpture of Mueck's father, often displayed lying on the floor of an exhibit, unadorned by cloth, casket, or context, is only a meter long—small enough, the artist has noted, to cradle in one's arms—and gives no hint at the life of the man memorialized in that lifeless body. *"Dead Dad* is a sculpture of monstrous loneliness," writes critic Heiner Bastian, and I believe the monstrosity of that loneliness comes from a body's inability to ever convey the true story of a father and a son, and from a son's inability to ever convey the true story of a memory that longs for a permanent burial.

Today my father and I live hundreds of miles apart and see each other once or twice a year. We try to keep in touch over the phone, but he's seventy years old now, and sometimes our conversations seem to increase rather than decrease the distance between us. He always asks about my boys, and my wife, and the weather, and sometimes we talk about a house project I'm working on or about the latest political upheaval, but eventually there will be a lull in the conversation, and if neither of us can think of anything more to say, we exchange "I love yous," and I thank him for calling. When we hang up, and I go about my day, I try hard not to imagine him alone on the other end of the line, holding the quiet phone in his lap.

Other times, though, we talk, and it's as if he's right in the room with me, and he's cracked open a case of wisdom and is pulling out little memories one by one, unwrapping them from their papers and passing them to me gently. And the few conversations we've had about his year in prison, conversations that I feared would be fraught with anger and dodging, have been our most open, most honest, and most satisfying. "It was the worst moment of my life," he told me. "I felt like my whole world was crashing down around me."

And to hear him talk of his pain, his shame, his sense of impotence at the perfect storm of wrong turns, misunderstandings, and lawyer missteps that ultimately led to his conviction was to see another myth fall away—an easy myth about my father as an emotionally unavailable man who struggles to relate to his kids—and in its place see my father emerge, a vulnerable man with a past he cannot change, who has, in his own way, been standing with his arms outstretched for a very long time.

And amidst all this, one memory is beginning to make sense. It is the memory of that first day visiting Dad at the halfway home when he asked me to punch him in the stomach. I'd thought he was joking around then, showing off, trying to prove something. I'd wanted to punch him because it was impressive to see him take the blows without a flinch, but now I think a different part of me was glad for the chance to hit him, and I'm all but certain a part of him was equally glad for the chance to take the hit.

Sometimes at night I call my father while I'm putting the boys to bed, and I prop the phone up on the edge of their bunk and put the receiver on speakerphone, and then I leave them to talk. For Grandpa, my boys are an outlet for all his happy stories, for his tales of life in the navy, of working as a sheriff's deputy in Las Vegas, of shooting wedding photography in the seventies in a powder-blue tux. They are a rapt audience, and they hang on every word. To my boys, Grandpa is still mythic, an ageless sage, a conduit to the past, a voice pointing them toward the future. And when I stand outside the room and listen to him talk, I'm glad that he has other stories to tell and glad that these are the stories my boys will know him by. And when they say good night and hang up the phone, I can't help but think of my own future, when these boys, who started out small enough to hold in the crook of my arm, will become men, and I will be the one calling on the weekends to hear their voices, looking for a place to park my stories, grasping for a way to reconnect with my sons.

Call Me Joey

As a graduate student at a professional writers' conference, standing in a buffet line that I hadn't paid to be in, next to real adults who had real jobs and real conference registrations that included lunch, I already felt out of place. I picked gingerly at the food on the table, trying not to draw attention to myself. A thirtysomething woman filling her plate beside me glanced in my direction and, perhaps sensing my discomfort, attempted some small talk. "'Joey'?" she said, looking down at my nametag. "You go by 'Joey,' huh?" I laughed and shrugged and stirred the salad and said something about my real name being Joseph, and how *Joey* is kind of, well, you know, what people have always called me, and then we exchanged niceties about our respective universities, and I handed her the salad tongs and walked away to find the kids' table.

I have been answering questions like that my entire adult life—friends and strangers alike wondering aloud at my choice to go by *Joey*. I think I understand their confusion. *Joe Cool, Joe College, Joe America, Joe Six-Pack, Joe the Plumber*—there's a certain blue-collar sexiness about *Joe*. But *Joey College*? *Joey Six-Pack*? *G. I. Joey*? Throw a *y* on the end, and what happens? That everyman sex appeal disappears, and you're left with nothing but your average Joey—cute, curly-headed, and cartoony.

Most of the Joeys I knew growing up, I knew from television. Think Joey Gladstone of *Full House*, Joey Tribbiani from *Friends*,

Joey Russo in *Blossom* (whoa!). I understood early on that *Joey* was a name for little kids, or at least, for kidlike people. Even the infamous Joey Buttafuoco, paramour of the Long Island Lolita and talk of every tabloid magazine from the early 1990s, seemed to give off an aura of harmless imbecility. Joeys were, as a rule, simple-minded baby faces that no one took seriously.

Consider the perpetually prepubescent Joey of *New Kids on the Block*, who joined the band just before his thirteenth birthday, taking his place beside neighborhood friends Donny and Danny, and brothers Jordan and Jonathan. According to *People* magazine, Joey signed on to sing the high notes "like Michael Jackson"—a fact that added to his childish persona.

I was in the fourth grade when I first saw the "fab five" silk-screened onto backpacks and Trapper Keepers at school— glossy, fresh faces of budding masculinity that made the girls around me swoon. They talked and dreamed and giggled about Jordan's sideburns, Donny's dimples, Danny's arms, Jonathan's hair, and maybe one or two even crushed a little on Joey's smooth skin, but when I looked at those photos, all I saw was the way the flash caught the peach fuzz on Joey's cheek and suspended it there, permanently.

I may have felt self-conscious about my slightly childish name in elementary school, but as I was still an actual child, my name invited little attention. Those with more peculiar names were not so lucky. I remember Wilford, the runny-nosed boy in the corner of my first-grade classroom forever pulling up the backside of his trousers; and Ella, the daughter of Russian immigrants whose real name was Elvira, though she made sure few people knew it; and Turaj, an Arab American who road my bus and eventually started calling himself "T. J." I imagine these classmates wore their names like bruises, covering them up, explaining them away, wishing people would ask about something else.

But even kids with less unusual names aren't safe. At the very first roll call of the year, when every teacher stumbles through a list of unfamiliar names, flattening out vowels that should be rounded and digging up consonants that should stay buried, all our names become the potential subject of public mutilation, scrutiny, and often ridicule. Emily, Andrew, and Christy don't usually have to worry, but Emil, Andréa, and Kirsten must forever be correcting, spelling out, and pronouncing. Morgan and Pat suffer the ignominy of gender-based misunderstandings, and every Rick and Virginia in the English-speaking world must surely put up with a ceaseless litany of explicit playground taunts.

Joey never earned me that kind of trouble as a kid, except maybe once—almost—when I accidentally got a flyer for Miss Teen USA in the mail addressed to "Jocy" Franklin, inviting me to enter the contest, and for a moment, standing on the porch with the flyer in hand, I feared my older brothers might find it and parade it around the house, the neighborhood, our school. I crumpled up the flyer and buried it in the bottom of the garbage can and prayed against further junk mail typos.

In high school I met a Joe who confirmed for me what I'd come to suspect about the name. He was a member of the speech and debate team and Model UN. He wore a black belt in Tae Kwan Do and took enough AP credits to start college as a sophomore. His jazz piano solos routinely brought audiences to tears, and every morning during advanced physics class, he finished most of the *New York Times* crossword by himself.

What's worse, I never heard him say a mean thing about anyone. He didn't drink. He didn't seem to care about impressing girls or playing the usual sports, and despite his participation in so many activities that would have meant social suicide for almost anyone else, he was surrounded by friends, including me. He was a Joe to the core, all class and cool, and I knew he was absolutely un-hate-able, and so I hated him for it. At least, a dark, jealous part of me must have. That would explain why, one inexplicable night, I dreamt of meeting him in the hallway of our school and blowing him away with a shotgun, a solitary blast from the hip. I woke up breathing heavy, sweating with relief that I hadn't just killed the only perfect boy I'd ever known.

Soon after starting college, I began to introduce myself as *Joe*, and though I thought I would feel the change like some kind of revelation, I mostly felt phony. I'd never been a *Joe*, never thought of myself as a *Joe*, and here I was parading around as if I were one. I'm sure the difference was too subtle for others to notice, but I still felt like I was wearing a hairpiece, trying to pull a fast one on the new people in my life. And the switch just ended up confusing them. As soon as they got to know me and my old circle of friends, and heard them call me "Joey," they would inevitably ask, "Which is it, 'Joey' or 'Joe'?"

I wish there had been an easier answer.

These are the dilemmas parents worry about when naming their children—or at least the dilemmas they should worry about. Each time that Melissa and I set out to name a baby, we knew we had to admit all our own hang-ups. We could never have a *Corey* because, well, I knew this guy named Corey, and he was a jerk; we could never have a *David* because Melissa dated a guy named David; *Jack* was out of the question because, according to her, *Jack* was a dirty-old-man name; and we could never have a *Tucker* because, well, think about it. And frankly, *Joe* was off the list because then our son would be Joe Jr., and Hollywood had ruined that name years ago. I was so arrested by the idea of choosing someone else's name—the power, responsibility, and finality of it all—that our oldest boy almost went home from the hospital "Baby Franklin." We ended up picking *Callan*, a name Melissa liked, and I didn't hate.

Most parents, thankfully, find protection in popularity, comfort in conformity. There will always be thousands of Jacobs, Michaels, Emilys, and Sarahs. But even with the volumes of available baby-naming literature that offer definitions, etymologies, suggestions, and cautionary tales of baby-naming disaster, a remarkable number of children end up with names like Kobe and Paris. A family in New Zealand actually named their daughter "Talula Does the Hula From Hawaii" and would have gotten away with it, too, if a judge hadn't forced them to change it.

Such names suggest that some parents worry more about what a name will mean for *them* than what it will mean for their child—the girl who has to explain that her parents were big fans of a spoiled reality television star, or the boy who has to tell people he's named after a professional athlete who was himself named after a type of Japanese beef, or that girl who had to wait until she was nine years old for a New Zealand family court to rule that her name constituted child abuse.

My own parents named me after Joseph, the biblical prophet, a visionary head-turner who saved all Egypt from famine—a feat that required him to talk his way out of slavery, prison, and the greedy fingers of a powerful, seductive woman. Not a bad namesake, if a little hard to live up to. And not at all uncommon, either. *Joseph* has been in the top one hundred baby names since the dawn of baby name statistics. Never at the very top, but always in the pack—in other words, a safe, comfortable choice for my parents—at least until they started calling me *Joey*.

Joseph is Hebrew, and depending on which baby name directory you check, it means "Jehovah gives increase," or "God will uplift." A Jewish friend tells me the Hebrew diminutive form is *Yossi*. But I think that when he signed official kingdom documents, Joseph of Egypt avoided writing *Yossi*, though I can imagine the pharaoh asking him one day, "Yosef? Your name, it sounds so formal. What does your wife call you at home?" If anyone could call back to earth "he whom God will uplift," it would have been his wife, who must have called him "Yossi" when no one else was around. Still, *Joseph* seems so unequivocally, heroically good, and the name so loaded with a particular confidence that I'm not sure a *Joey* can emulate.

Perhaps my childish name has given me a head start on the Christian mandate to "become as a little child." The New Testament is full of Josephs who deferred their own interests for God's Kingdom. The young Joseph of Nazareth, descendent of King David and rightful heir to the throne of Israel, chose to shrug the Mosaic mandate concerning unfaithful wives and, shouldering the weight of the Nazareth rumor mill, wedded the expectant Virgin Mary. Another Joseph from farther south in Arimathea risked political life and limb by stealing away "in secret" to "boldly" beg Pilate for the body of Jesus. That Joseph took Jesus' body to his own freshly hewn tomb and laid it to rest.

Then there is Joseph, the younger brother of Jesus. Disciple. Friend. Confidant? I imagine quiet discussions in the evening away from the hungry throng, little brother Joseph listening quietly as big brother Jesus talked of his forty days in the wilderness, of the look on their mother's face when the water in those barrels became wine, of the whip he made, and the way the money changers scattered in the temple. It may have taken Joseph a long time to accept his brother's public identity and what that identity meant for his own aspirations. I wonder whether Peter, James, and John called him "Yossi" when they came to visit, and I wonder whether the nickname made little Joseph bristle. One day when the two brothers were children, their mother, Mary, may have walked out of the house to find them wrestling in the grass. She would have called to them, stood them up, and as she brushed the dirt from their clothes, little Yossi may have pointed at his older brother and said, "He started it." And Mary would have looked at her young child and said, "Yossi, Yossi," shaking her head, because they both knew that Jesus never "started it."

All diminutive names are childish. But often they are also intimate—brief and telling names passed between lovers, brothers, and childhood friends. Perhaps when a person chooses to hang on to a name like Billy or Mikey, they choose to hang on to a bit of childhood, a bit of innocence, and reject a certain amount of the formality and posturing that so muddles the adult world. Children, after all, will tell you their deepest secrets, their darkest fears, their greatest joys. They'll talk to strangers in line at the grocery store, dip their graham cracker in their friend's milk, run down the hall naked waving their towels behind them. Everyone is uncle, aunt, cousin. Everyone is huggable. Befriendable. When I asked my mother how the family had decided to call me *Joey* instead of *Joseph*, she laughed and said, "Who could look at a little baby like you and call him 'Joseph'?" and she said the name with a deep, affected seriousness.

Outside of names like *Adolf* and *Bubba*, and maybe *Candy*, names and their connotations aren't really that static, even if I'm afraid they are. Take some Josephs from more recent history. In the first half of the last century, Joseph Stalin raked across the Russian countryside, communizing and cajoling his way to an infamy crowned by the murder, imprisonment, and oppression of millions of his own people. And on the other side of the Atlantic, Senator Joe McCarthy personified midcentury Red Scare paranoia in the United States—a reaction based in part on fears generated by men like Stalin.

In the 1950s and 1960s, New York mobster Joey Gallo, immortalized in the eponymous Bob Dylan song, tried to take over the Colombo mob family and was thanked for his efforts by two gunmen during a birthday celebration in Little Italy.

And I don't know what to do with Joseph Paul Franklin, a man with a name so close to my own that it startled me the first time I saw it. A racist serial killer with an affinity for sniper gear and Nazi dogma, Franklin went on a three-year killing spree from Miami to Cincinnati to Salt Lake City, targeting interracial couples and civil rights leaders. The rampage did not end until more than twenty had been killed, and Franklin was finally arrested on October 28, 1980—less than two weeks before I was born.

In the twelve days between his arrest and the day of my birth, the *Washington Post* ran five articles on Joseph Franklin, and the *New York Times* ran twelve. The Associated Press put out no fewer than twenty-four news wires on the killer, and those wires were picked up by who knows how many local and regional papers. Joseph Franklin was extradited to Salt Lake City on November 6. On November 10, the day I was born, the day my parents made my name official, newspapers across the country ran stories about the unfolding events of Joseph Franklin's atrocities. For my parents, who'd heard only snippets of news coverage about the killings, the name *Joseph Franklin* maintained its satisfying allusion to biblical loyalty, sacrifice, and faith. But for families of the victims, my name must bring up the worst of memories—gunfire, the ringing of a phone, the cottony air in a funeral home, the void in a room you can't ever get used to.

What's interesting is this: Franklin's real name was James Clayton Vaughn, and changing his name appears to have been a crucial part of the preparation for his killing spree. He took his new name from founding father Benjamin Franklin and Nazi propaganda minister Paul Joseph Goebbels, but he inverted the first and middle names. What was it about the name *Joseph* that he felt would do him justice, that he felt would erase some part of his past and help him step into his new, violent future?

My attempts to change my name from *Joey* to *Joe* never went anywhere. I eventually resigned myself to the diminutive form, and imagined I was embracing it as a bald man embraces his hair loss (something else I've had to deal with). If bald could be beautiful, then *Joey* could be a respectable, adultish name that I could pass along to strangers at a conference without glancing down to make sure my tie wasn't stained with macaroni and cheese.

Joe Plicka, a fiction writer and friend of mine who also went by *Joey* most of his childhood, had better luck than I did shaking the nickname. Born Joseph Benjamin Plicka, he was the fifth Joseph in a line trailing back to the peasant fields of Moravia. His mother never called him Joey, never wanted to call him Joey, and certainly never expected him to go off to his first day of kindergarten and come home with a new name, but that is exactly what happened. Two other Josephs stood ahead of him in the alphabet, and when his name was called that first day, his befuddled teacher suggested he try something else, for her sake. Apparently, though he has no recollection of the decision, he said, "Call me 'Joey,'" and the name stuck. Like me, he grew up in the shadow of the goofy, bumbling sitcom Joeys and squirmed every time he heard the name Joey Buttafuoco on the news. Like me, he saw college as an opportunity to reinvent himself, and, like me, the first few times he introduced himself as Joe, it felt awkward.

But, unlike me, Joe Plicka managed to make the name fit, and the change apparently made quite a difference. The way he explains it, switching to *Joe* gave him instant social capital that he spent on changing his own preconceived notion of who he was. He started reading serious books and chasing seriously good-looking women. He picked up a guitar and joined a band. In short, he became an independent adult, done with the childishness of his name and the mindset that came with it.

Joe is more than a decade out of high school and has been married for nearly five years to Emily, who has known him only as a *Joe*, but occasionally at home she calls him by his old nickname, and she's amused when old friends call on the phone for "Joey." Their first child was a girl, but a few years ago they had a boy—a curly-headed fireplug with a sprouting cleft chin and a wry, calculating smile. They named him Joseph. Joseph the sixth. And though Joe almost always calls his son by his full name, Emily is in love with *Joey*—"just while he's a little boy," she says.

Someday their little Joey will stand at the edge of adulthood and will have to decide what to do about his name and all it potentially stands for. But will that moment be any different than it is for the Billys and Jimmys and Mikeys in the world standing on the edge of the same decision? Certainly it won't be on a par with the problems of kids named Cornelius or Chastity or Talula Does the Hula, but part of me likes to think there's something unique about the Joey dilemma, even if that *something* is how the name occasionally makes me feel like I've got my shirt tucked into my underwear.

Little More Than Strangers

McCarran International Airport in Las Vegas, Nevada. It's a quarter after six on a Sunday morning, and the slots are ringing in the background as a few dozen passengers slouch in their seats waiting for their flights. I sit holding my bag in my lap, taking mental note of my wallet, passport, boarding pass, and cash. I check the lid of my water bottle, curl my toes inside my shoes, and shift my weight in my seat. The terminal is quiet. If not for the slot machines in the background, we could be in a library, a hospital waiting room, a funeral home. Several more passengers arrive in the terminal, but the seat next to me remains empty until a smartly dressed woman in a gray pantsuit and silver hoop earrings wheels her luggage into the sitting area and collapses at my side. Her hair is a sculpture, with precise black curls tucked neatly behind her ears. She is on business, I think. Sales, maybe, or consulting, and I can't imagine how early she must have woken up this morning for her hair to look that good. I say hello, and her lips flinch in a non-committal smile. She says hi under her breath and turns away, rests her immaculate head on top of her purse, and appears to fall asleep. The sound of slot machines still rings in the air, and I have the sudden urge to write down a note about this woman sitting next to me and the impossibility of her perfect hair.

So I get up. To look for a pen.

I've cultivated a good habit of jotting down notes when thoughts come to me, but not such a good habit of keeping pens around. And every time I find myself in want of one, I remember Brian Doyle, who said that a writer "always carries two pens, a prime pen and a backup in case of emergencies," and then I think about a writer friend of mine who always carries two pens (blue Paper Mate Write Bros.) along with a folded sheet of paper in his back pocket. I even started the day with a pen that I'd taken from my parents' house, but it disappeared somewhere between the car and the terminal. Still, I feel that writerly urge to jot down a note about this woman, and if I want to take a note, I have to find a pen.

The gift shop, it turns out, does not sell pens. I can buy a Kit Kat, a Coke, or an "I ♥ Las Vegas" T-shirt, but I cannot buy a pen. I figure the clerk might have one she can spare, so I linger a moment looking puzzled after she's explained her lack of pens, hoping she will open her drawer and pull one out for me, but she turns away as soon as she's answered my question, and I am left to walk back through the gift shop past the mugs and folded sweaters and rows of magazines.

Out in the terminal hallway a woman in a Southwest Airlines polo stands at a kiosk advertising credit cards. From this woman I learn all about the risk-free, no-obligation card and the free flights and bonus points I can get for signing up, and how I have to sign up today if I want the free flights. She doesn't know I am only talking to her because I need a pen, and she has at least three at her kiosk, and I know she is only talking to me because she wants to sell me a credit card. I tell her I'll think about the card, and I ask her for a pen. To my surprise, she opens up a drawer in the kiosk and pulls out a box of orphaned pens for me to choose from. I take a yellow pen with a pocket clip and an advertisement printed on its side for the "Brooks Stone Ranch in New Braunfels, Texas" and a phone number: 830-624-7554.

Back at my seat, the woman with immaculate hair sleeps on, and I sit down with my notebook. I wonder about the Brooks Stone Ranch—and how a pen from New Braunfels, Texas, ends up in a kiosk at the Las Vegas Airport in an old box full of misplaced pens. I wonder who brought it here, whether they were in Vegas on business or pleasure, whether Vegas was worth it or not, what "Braunfels" means, and who might be on the other end of that phone line.

I pull out my cell phone and dial the number. It is now close to eight o'clock in the morning, Texas time, on a Sunday. The phone rings, and I rehearse what I might say to whoever answers the phone—*Hi, my name is Joey, and I'm a writer, and I just found a pen advertising your ranch, and I'm sitting in the Las Vegas airport terminal surrounded by complete strangers who are perfectly content to stare at their magazines or sleep on their palms or type away on their computers and smartphones, and it's got me thinking about the bubbles we all walk around in, and so I'm calling to get out of my bubble, and I know it's early on a Sunday, and I knew chances were slim that anyone would even pick up, but here you are, and we're talking, so maybe could you tell me a little about your ranch operation and whether you specialize in cattle or tourists or both. And what does "Braunfels" mean? And do you have any children, and when was the last time you spoke with them, and did you think when you were young, say about thirty-three, that you would miss them as much as you do now? And how are you? I mean really? Because I hate that question and the way I throw it around with people, and the way I answer it—"fine," "great," "wonderful"—when really, sometimes it's not fine, great, or wonderful. Sometimes I want to say, "life sucks," that my wife doesn't appreciate me, that my kids won't stop pinching one another, that my left elbow keeps flaring up so I can't lean on it. But I hate that kind of answer, too—with its self-indulgent woe-is-me mentality. I mean, who am I to complain, right? Hello?*

The phone rings and rings, and finally I hang up. Sunday morning on a ranch—everyone must be asleep. Asleep like the woman beside me with the impossibly perfect hair. I put away my phone, and she begins to stir in her seat. She looks at me and smiles and says, "Would you make sure I'm awake if they start to board?" She gestures at the ticket counter.

"Sure," I say, and she puts her head back on her bag and slips back into sleep, and I put away my phone, delighted to have an assignment.

The waiting area has grown quite full by now, and my sleeping charge and I are almost completely surrounded by other travelers. Across from me sits an elderly man in khaki slacks and a loud plaid shirt. He hides behind a copy of the *Las Vegas Review Journal*. To my left, an Indian couple eats breakfast out of a bag from McDonald's. The man is in blue jeans and a polo, the woman wears a maroon sari and a *tilaka* mark on her forehead. A few feet from me stands a man wearing oversized jean shorts and tight braids in his hair. He wears a pair of large headphones designed so the speakers look like hamburgers on either side of his head. He appears lost in his music, the rest of the world canceled out by his noise-canceling headphones.

The call for boarding rings out over the intercom, and everyone begins to mobilize. The Indian couple crumples their McDonald's bag and discards it. The old man in the khaki shorts folds his paper and slides it into a zippered pocket of his suitcase. The man with the headphones pulls his bag off the ground and begins gathering himself to line up. I double-check my passport, my wallet, and my water bottle, and stand up to get in line at the gate, completely forgetting my wake-me-up assignment from the woman with the perfect hair. I leave her asleep in her seat, and by the time I realize my mistake, I am already moving forward in line, boarding pass in hand. When I look back to the sitting area, she is gone, swallowed up by the crowd. At least, I tell myself, she won't miss her flight.

Buckling into my seat as other passengers board the plane, I keep an eye out for the woman with the perfect hair, half hoping for a chance to apologize and half hoping to avoid another meeting, but she never makes it down to my end of the aircraft. Instead the plane slowly fills until just a few seats remain, including one at my side and one in the row behind me. Two college-aged girls—obviously friends and obviously wanting to sit by one another—stand in the aisle in front of me, looking puzzled as they stare at the two separated empty seats, and then they look at me.

Giving up my seat for these two girls puts me one row back between a quiet Asian woman in black tights and an excessively tan, thirtysomething man wearing plaid shorts and a long-sleeved T-shirt. Both of them are engrossed in their phones when I pardon myself and take my seat between them. The man says hello, and the woman nods her head, then they both return to their phones. I slide my bag under the seat in front of me and then look to my left and to my right, sizing up my seatmates.

The Asian woman—with her shoulders turned in and her head bent over her phone, her long black hair hanging over either side of her face—might as well have been the Great Wall of China, so I turn to the excessively tan man and ask him whether he's heading out or heading home. Home, he says, and then offers an enthusiastic appraisal of the Las Vegas nightlife and the bachelor party he attended the night before.

"It was everything a bachelor party is supposed to be," he says with what I think is a knowing smile, the kind that might have accompanied raised eyebrows and a wink if the man were, say, a fifteen-year-old boy. But since I've had about as much experience at bachelor parties as your average fifteen-year-old, I use the few sitcom references I can recall and conjure an image of this stranger in the back room of some bar surrounded by awkward men holding beers while they watch a bikini-clad stripper strut circles around their soon-to-be married friend. The man doesn't elaborate, however, except to say something about the whole night being a little foggy and to repeat his affection for the city. He asks about me in the polite, disinterested way air travelers are wont to do, and I tell him I am an English teacher. "Oh," he says in way that I know means I just killed whatever buzz had been lingering from the night before, and he puts on his headphones and looks out the window with what could only be described as a measure of wistfulness mixed with hangover and injected with a supersaturation of small talk.

The plane soon takes off, and as we rise into the air, I notice that the Asian woman beside me has fallen asleep. Her head bobs with the motion of the plane, and her phone has started slipping through her fingers. When it finally falls out of her hand, she jerks awake and looks around, briefly, as if hoping no one has seen her, and then she puts her phone away and settles back into her nap. With no one to talk to, I pull out my laptop to get a little work done, doing my best to honor the unspoken etiquette of airplane personal space. I keep my elbows tucked in at my sides and my knees together. I give up as much of both armrests as I can, direct my air vent away from my neighbors, and keep my light off.

As I type though, I notice in my peripheral vision that the Asian woman's black hair is drawing closer and closer to my own head. In her exhaustion she is leaning unconsciously toward me. I lower my shoulder to give her room to lean, and after a few moments with her head pitched awkwardly in my direction, she bolts upright, glancing at me out of the corner of her eye, searching, I imagine, for any sign of how far she'd been leaning over. I keep typing, pretending not to notice her bewildered look, and after a few seconds, she is bobbing again, her head slipping down toward me and then back up, never quite aloft and never quite fallen over, and she keeps on bobbing like this for several minutes. I drop my shoulder lower and lower to save her the embarrassment of making contact, and we fly on like this for a good half hour, she leaning and I slouching, doing my best to preserve the space between us without waking her up.

My inner dialogue during this awkward dance between her nodding, unconscious head and my slouching, self-conscious shoulder goes something like this:

"She's ridiculous."

"She's probably exhausted."

"Probably hungover."

"I hate to wake her up."

"If she could see us, she'd be mortified."

"What am I supposed to do, jab her in the ribs?"

"My back is getting sore."

"She could rest on my shoulder."

"What if she gets the wrong idea?"

"What if I have to slouch like this for another hour?"

"Oh, forget it."

I ease myself up ever so slowly and let her head come in for a landing on my shoulder. She doesn't move at first, but then she adjusts her head slightly, as if unconsciously accepting the gesture, and I try to hold still and let her sleep. I sit and watch the plane's cabin in front of me, only the backs of heads visible above the blue leather seats, little bumps like braille I can't read or, perhaps, like prairie dog mounds—small signs of life that suggest an entire world hidden beneath the surface. Our heads bob in concert with the light turbulence vibrating through the aircraft, and it occurs to me that my own head, seen from behind, appears just as anonymous to the people sitting behind me.

Soon flight attendants will rise and walk down the aisle collecting orders for small plastic cups of juice, soda, or coffee, and the pilot will turn off the seatbelt sign, and lines will begin to form at the restrooms, and some of us will read or sleep or chat with our neighbors. In approximately thirty minutes, an exhausted Asian woman will wake up, realize she's been sleeping on my shoulder for who-knows-how-long, and she will not be able to make eye contact or acknowledge me in any way for the rest of the flight. When we land she will hurry to the exit without looking back, and I will never see her again. But right now in the early hum of this short flight, I will keep still, she will sleep soundly, and the two of us will, for a moment, be a little more than strangers.

My Hair Piece

My brother Jason and I stood shirtless in front of the bathroom mirror together, squeezing zits, counting chest hairs, and pulling faces to make each other laugh. I was thirteen, and he was sixteen, and the difference showed in our biceps, on our chins, and in the way we fixed our hair. If I combed mine in the morning, it mopped out by lunch, but even at dinner Jason's held strong, a coiffure of teenage brilliance born from the teeth of a Ping-Pong-paddle-sized brush and held in place by half a can of Mom's Aqua Net. A metrosexual before his time, Jason treated his hair as some musicians treat their instruments—with an artist's careful hand and a lover's gentle touch.

But at night, in front of the mirror in our bathroom, he loosened up a bit. We ratted our fingers through our hair; we brushed it out wildly; we cocked our jaws at odd angles and stretched the tendons in our necks; we shrugged our shoulders to our ears and flared our nostrils. Our growing bodies were forever novel, and every day we found a new gesture or contortion that left us giddy, amazed at the absurdity of our changing flesh, curled over in laughter at our own gangly pubescence.

We eventually washed our faces and said good night, but I often stayed behind and continued picking, flexing, and imagining, as if I could will myself a little taller, a little stronger, a little hairier in the right places. Our contortions were funny, but something about them stung. Especially the goofy hair. I wetted mine down and parted it on one side, then the other, then down the middle. I even spiked it with gel, but nothing seemed to work. I leaned in close and stared at the skin on my face, wondering when stubble would finally begin to grow. Jason was already shaving, and I'd noticed sideburns slowly creeping down his cheeks. I squinted, and then lifted my eyebrows. I puffed out my cheeks to feel the skin stretch around my jaw, furrowed my brow, and opened my mouth wide. Then I pulled my hair back to examine the real problem.

I'd been suspecting it for a while, eyeing my forehead warily during these solo sessions in front of the bathroom mirror. I stared at the fearful frontline of wispy hair whose retreat had already rendered my oldest brother, my father, all my uncles, and both my grandfathers as bald as bass drums. Was this the forehead they saw in the mirror at thirteen, I wondered. I told myself that my hair was thicker, hardier, more like Jason's. It was a delusion that sounded good to me, and so I let it play. But somewhere in the back of my mind, I knew fate had pulled reality from its traveling case, looped the strap around his neck, and begun tuning the strings. And yet, the sound of that swan song was so far off that I convinced myself I couldn't really hear it.

By the time I turned fifteen, I could no longer pretend, not with the mounting hair in my comb, in my hat, and on my morning pillow. Still, I resisted. I counted hairs and looked up statistics on average daily shedding. I scanned old photographs to compare hairlines past and present. I looked up the definition of widow's peak and convinced myself that maybe I'd been worrying about nothing more than a genetically inherited point in my hairline. I tried marking that hairline with Mom's eyeliner to gauge any loss over time, but I couldn't draw a line faint enough to go unnoticed without it washing off in the shower. I stopped wearing baseball hats, just in case. I combed my hair every night before bed because I heard that combing stimulated the roots. I seriously contemplated Rogaine and watched Hair Club for Men commercials with embarrassing earnestness. I feared losing my hair like a sheep might fear castration if it knew to look out for the farmer and his pliers. Like beer gut and back hair, balding was, I'd convinced myself, a death knell for male sex appeal, an emasculating inevitability tolling in my ears.

His junior year in high school, Jason grew full-blown sideburns and started learning the harmonica, so he could play backup for his friend's garage band. He bought himself a few harps— black and silver Lee Oscars keyed in C, D, and E—and he sat in his room with the door closed and listened to a cassette called *Harpin' It Easy*. From outside his room I could hear the click and smack of spit and dry lips as he mimicked the instructor playing different licks. He learned to draw and blow and eventually to curl his tongue back into his mouth and bend notes, and over time his sideburns grew and curled into handlebars on his cheeks, and his hair turned wild and thick, and he started wearing long johns under his T-shirts. He bought a pair of Vans and some hemp jewelry. He started listening to bands like Led Zeppelin and Counting Crows, and began playing music of his own—deep and guttural blues and rock recorded on his friend's second-hand four-track.

Music seemed a hair tonic for my brother, so I decided to learn the harmonica, too. Jason gave me an old, dented Lee Oscar and let me borrow *Harpin' It Easy*. And it should have been easy, I imagined. What are the blues, after all, if not a channel for loss? My anxiety about balding may not have been enough to launch a career, but it ought to at least have helped coax out a few soulful riffs.

Jason's voluminous hair and immutable sideburns loomed large in my mind during those first attempts at twelve-bar blues. I learned to hear the rolling rhythm, to curl and bend the notes, but I couldn't quite master the sound. I picked up some albums from the record store to study, and I even looked for help in a book titled *Harmonica for the Musically Hopeless*. Eventually

I learned to play "Oh! Susanna" and a few other folk songs, but the blues were as hard coming as the pepper flakes of hair dusting my cheeks, the slight hint of sideburns that were never quite thick enough, never quite "there" enough to do much more than make my face look dirty.

Still, I learned to recognize the gravelly coolness of Muddy Waters and B. B. King, of Jimmy Rogers and John Lee Hooker, and though I got lost trying to play along with songs like "Boom Boom" and "Lucille," I found comfort in the call and repeat of the refrains, all that melancholy and doubt packaged up as confidence—or was it the other way around? I couldn't really tell, but at that point, in my brother's shadow, it didn't really matter.

During the fall of my senior year in high school, I made a trip to Supercuts that removed all doubt about my receding hairline. Lucy, the spritely stylist who attended me, stood just a hair over five feet tall and spoke with an ambiguous East Asian accent. Her hair, an immaculate tangle of sculpting products and bobby pins, hung around her face like scaffolding. Razor-blade eyebrows darted across her forehead, leaving streaks of blue eye shadow in their wake, and her high cheekbones glowed with bull's-eyes of red rouge.

"I'm getting my senior pictures taken next week," I told her. "I figured I ought to see a professional."

Lucy smiled through shimmering red lipstick and tied a black cape around my neck, saying something like, "We make you look handsome. Very handsome," apparently pleased that I considered her and Supercuts "professional."

Lucy refused to use the electric clippers, scoffing at them in their holster on the counter as if they were training wheels or sheet music she'd long since memorized. Instead, she pulled out a thin pair of scissors and began to work her way around my head, pulling my hair tightly between her fingers as she cut. Then she pulled out another pair of scissors bladed with steel-comb teeth. And then another comb and yet another pair of scissors. She moved with a preternatural, syncopated rhythm, her scissors slowing down and speeding up, rising and falling as she turned a slow circle around my head. We were engrossed, she in her work, and I in the blur of her hands and the snip-clink of cut and comb. She returned to her first set of scissors, but this time she guided her cuts with a large arced comb, pulling it from my forehead straight back to the base of my neck, a slow, methodical coda, checking for symmetry, balance, and taper. And just when I thought she'd finished, she reached inside her drawer once more and pulled out a small, electric beard trimmer, her finale. "Almost done," she said, and she began to clean up all my edges. She zipped and nipped every out-of-place hair she could find, and then she stopped at my forehead, furrowed her brow, and said, "You're too young to have a widow's peak," and without hesitating or asking my permission, she shaved my hairline even.

I'd like to say this was a horrifying moment—an existential crisis that forced me to accept my own mortality—but instead of feeling anxious about my hair and angry about Lucy's barbershop bravado, I felt something akin to liberation. Up to that point, I'd been looking in the mirror, trying to see Jason in my own reflection, and now, thanks to Lucy, for the first time that mirror gave me someone else to look at. Someone who could buy a pair of clippers and cut his own hair in his bathroom, someone who could stop worrying about all that hair in the shower, who could give up trying so hard to be someone he was not. I felt a strange, fledgling confidence all packaged up in uncertainty and apprehension—or was it the other way around? I couldn't tell, but at that point, with my newfound reflection looking back at me in the mirror, it didn't really matter.

My liberation lasted only a few weeks. Shortly after the Supercuts incident, everyone around me began to take notice. At nineteen, just before leaving on a mission trip to Japan for two years, my friend Kevin asked me, "So, do you think you'll have any hair when you get back?"

It got worse once I arrived in Japan. When people guessed my age, they almost always said thirty or thirty-five. One woman actually said forty. During the New Year's holiday, instead of saying "*Akemashite omedeto*," which means Happy New Year, some of my friends said, "*Hagemashite omedoto*," which means "Congratulations, you're going bald."

Just before returning to the United States, another friend gave me this warning: "You should find a wife really quick when you get home, before she finds out you're balding."

And back in the States, when I met my wife, her teenage sister told her, "I don't think I could marry someone who was losing his hair like that."

Somehow coming to terms with my own baldness gave permission for the rest of the world to acknowledge it as well. Yet if I ever acknowledged my own hair loss, people would say, "What, you're not losing that much hair," or "I can't even tell," as if conspiring in denial somehow made it okay. I felt obliged to lean over and remove all doubt, pretended or otherwise. By then, the back of my head had thinned so much that from a distance it looked like I was wearing a skullcap.

"Oh, well," people said. "It could be worse."

Of course it could, I wanted to say, but all I could manage to conjure were a few of my father's bald jokes: "I didn't go bald, my hair just migrated south," I might say. Or, "Sure I'm going bald, because brains and hair don't grow well together," or perhaps my favorite: "The only bad part about going bald is not knowing when to stop washing your face." Of course, I prefaced these jokes with the disclaimer, "You know, my dad always said . . ." as if that granted me permission to repeat lame jokes with social impunity, as if invoking my father could somehow veil my own clamor for pity.

Today, my brother Jason—still taller and hairier than I am, and showing no signs of slowing down—has begun experimenting with his hair à la David Beckham and Colin Farrell. He still has the same Ping-Pong-paddle brush, but between girlfriends and professional stylists he's learned to use a variety of specialty shampoos, working waxes, defining pastes, and styling gels. Striving toward some fashion magnum opus that I will never understand, he sculpts and plays his hair to the point that I sometimes don't recognize him at first glance. He's moved on from harmonica-playing high school grunge god to business-traveling sales professional, and the number of coworkers and bank tellers—male and female—who frequently hit on him stands as a testament to the dizzying heights of his fashion presence.

I, meanwhile, still cut my hair in my bathroom with electric clippers and watch fewer and fewer strands fall into the sink each month. I haven't been to a barbershop in years, and one bottle of Suave lasts me months. Occasionally, when I lean over to tie my shoe or get something out of a bottom cupboard, my wife says, in passing, "You know, I almost forget you're even going bald, until you bend over like that."

My son Callan pats my head and says, "Dad, where did your hair go?"

And on occasion, I still pick up the harmonica, take a deep breath, and let loose the few clunky licks that I haven't forgotten. Nowadays, though, with the harp to my lips, I don't feel like I'm bending and reaching for the same impossible "coolness" I once was. But the notes still bend and my lips still smack, and if I let it, the music still conjures in me a slack-shouldered confidence and an unshakable blues, a contradiction that I've begun to realize is no contradiction at all.

One day recently at Jason's house, we found ourselves in front of the bathroom mirror with our boys brushing teeth and doing hair, getting ready to go out. Jason was piling a waxy goop in his hands and running it through his son's hair, giving it spikes here and there. Callan stood beside his cousin, hopping on one foot in anticipation. I'd just given Jason a green light to spike Callan's blond mop into something presentable. With both hands full of goop and hair, Jason turned to me and said, "You know, if you would grow your hair out," he paused for dramatic effect, "we could have some real fun with it."

"I don't think so," I said, and I sensed some pity on his face as he continued working gel into my son's hair. But I don't think he understood. I'm not interested in my hair being anything more than a confession of reality, a talisman against delusion, a bluesy refrain—less "I Got My Mojo Workin'" and more "The Thrill Is Gone."

We finished grooming our boys and followed them out of the bathroom, their spiky heads bobbing in front of us, and my son shouting something about "cool hair" and "Uncle Jason," and I patted him on the shoulder and thought to myself, "Enjoy it while it lasts, kid, . . . enjoy it while it lasts."

Houseguest

I found a cockroach on the first afternoon in our new house. He surprised me, peeking out from beneath the lip of the toe-kicked kitchen cabinets, watching my back as I washed dishes in a still-unfamiliar sink. It was late afternoon, and I'd taken a break from unpacking boxes to clean up the kitchen. My wife, Melissa, and I had just put money down on 1,200 square feet of sculpted shag carpet and peeling paint, and the place still felt like someone else's home. As I stood at the sink scrubbing dishes, my eye caught something small and black creeping across the floor. I thought it was a beetle at first, but when I pulled a paper towel from the roll and turned around, he darted across the room at roach speed—a greasy, twitching blur. He made a break for the gap between the cabinet and the fridge, but I reached down and caught him with the towel. A beetle I would have taken out back and set free in the yard; a beetle knows how to take a hint, will accept the eviction standing on its own six feet. But a cockroach is different: he'll glare up at you through the crumpled paper towel, his six crooked legs pawing at the air, long antennae waving back and forth like sabers. If he could spit at you, he would, or he'd play dead to fool you and then squirm out of your hands and dive under the fridge. I couldn't let him go. Instead, I shrouded his body with the paper towel and squished him between my fingers—twice. The first time too gently, and he kept struggling. The second time, just enough to feel him pop.

I say "him," but I have no way of knowing whether or not that roach was male or female. It usually takes an entomologist to tell them apart, and even roaches themselves depend largely on pheromones to find a date. Either way, I like to think of all cockroaches as male, the worst kind of male: dirty-uncle types who wear pit-stained T-shirts and smoke cigars while they sit wide-legged on your couch, talking loudly, drinking theatrically, and hitting on your girlfriend—bugs that put the creep in creepy.

Not exactly what I had in mind as our first houseguest.

My wife found another roach later that first night. She'd gotten up to get a drink of water, and when she climbed back in bed next to me, she put her head on the pillow and said, "There's a very large cockroach trapped out there for you to kill in the morning."

When I woke up and went out to the kitchen, I found the roach in front of the refrigerator, trapped beneath an upturned plastic cup. I kneeled down and peered at him, his hard body poised at the edge of his cell. Was he tired from turning circles all night, or had he just been sitting there waiting? Perhaps he'd been as surprised to see Melissa as Melissa was to see him. This house had, after all, been vacant for nearly six months. Perhaps after the old couple and all their things were finally hauled away, this roach and his cousins had emerged from the shadows to feed on the hair and toenails and crumbs that remained in the carpet—a feast to last a millennium if we hadn't shown up with our paper towels and plastic cups.

At more than an inch long, my prisoner was far too big to comfortably crush in a paper towel, so I found a shoe lying on the floor and lifted the cup. When the roach made a run for it, I brought the shoe down quickly, but I missed. He cut one way and then another. I struck three more times before hitting the roach, his broken body turned sideways in the carpet, his pointy legs bent unnaturally, his mandibles splayed and still. I picked him up with a tissue and threw him in the garbage and then turned on the sink, eager to wash my hands.

Cockroaches have a lot going for them in the make-me-scream-like-a-little-girl category. Most bugs elicit a fight-or-flight response of some kind, but the effect of the cockroach is particularly potent. They can be impossibly large or so tiny you can barely see them. They can shimmy across my living room at 80 cm per second, turn on a pinhead, and be under the couch before I have a chance to blink. They eat just about anything but can live for months without food. They carry diseases, allergens, and unpleasant odors. They appear out of nowhere, feed on my garbage, breed between the walls, and leave a trail of excrement wherever they go. They are the stuff of B-horror films, an entomological "other" few can find any reason to appreciate. Cockroaches are what entomologists call "uncharismatic"—as in, if a roach species were to suddenly become endangered, they would be hard-pressed to find donors for a "save the roaches" campaign, even among the hardiest members of the Sierra Club. Nobody cries when you kill a cockroach.

The woman who sold us this house broke down in tears shortly after signing the paperwork. We hadn't expected to see her, but there she was, holding her husband's hand in the lobby of the title office, wiping her eyes as she told us how hard it had been to go through with the deal, how sad she felt about leaving behind the house she grew up in, the house in which her parents had started and ended their lives together. She asked about our boys and told us how happy her parents would have been to see small children playing in the yard once more. I appreciated the sentiment, but if it lessened my desire to wipe the place clean, I didn't notice. The house had been a good find—like a vintage suit on a thrift-store rack. But this old woman's memories weren't what I wanted to hear just before we moved in. After all, no one who buys a suit from the thrift store wants to know about the guy who used to wear it.

We got started as soon as we moved in, tearing out faded floral shelf paper and old, cracked linoleum. We pulled up what carpet we could afford to replace and shampooed what was left behind. We ripped up chipping baseboards, stopped leaky drains, pulled stubborn nails, fixed broken doors, and laid new flooring in the kitchen. Outside, we threw away carloads of junk from the shed, trimmed wild hedges, fixed holes in the fence, and found ourselves occasionally staring in disbelief at what had once been the back lawn but was now a feral patch of weeds growing atop a carpet of lava rock and river stone. I raked and shoveled and Weedwacked, but mostly I just stood and looked at the yard, cursing the old couple and the mess of rocks they'd left behind.

And yet despite all the work, we were cooking meals in the kitchen and watching our boys dig holes in the garden. We were opening windows on sunny mornings to let in the breeze, and I was raking leaves out front each Saturday, enjoying the satisfaction of that regular suburban ritual. And I might even say we were settling in if it weren't for the persistent signs of our unwanted guests—roach droppings that fell from behind the walls like coffee grinds when I pulled back a baseboard; egg casings in neat rows under toolboxes in the shed; carcasses dried out beneath the fridge, behind the washing machine, and under the sink. We had roaches hiding behind our toilet, poking out of a hole in the wall near a drain pipe, and shooting across the floor when I pulled up a rug. Even in the backyard as I pushed dirt around, I'd occasionally see a roach in the weeds, slowly creeping toward the house. We may have startled the roaches by moving in, beat them back a bit with all our remodeling, but the truth was they were here first, and they weren't going without a fight.

There are many ways to rid your home of a cockroach infestation: sprays, gels, powders, sticky papers, and our weapon of choice—the roach motel. These little black traps contain poisons that put a snared roach to a slow death, allowing him to return to the nest where he defecates and dies, leaving his own contaminated fecal matter and carcass for his family to devour and, in turn, die slow, suffocating deaths themselves. The most common traps contain a variety of poisons in a base of peanut butter. A series of cardboard traps sold in Japan features cartoon roaches hanging out of cartoon windows, beckoning gently with tiny cartoon hands. Some researchers have even experimented mixing poison with synthetic versions of cockroach pheromones to lure unsuspecting males, creating what one BBC reporter called cockroach STDs.

When Melissa brought home traps, we divided them between us and split up to place them around the house in all the locations we'd seen roaches: under the fridge; behind the toilet and washing machine; and in select corners of the kitchen, bathroom, and our bedroom.

"That ought to do it," I said as I placed my last trap. Now all we had to do was wait for the roaches to make their move.

Young cockroaches scurry. They forage. They climb about, stretch their legs, follow trails, get into trouble, and mate like crazy. It takes several years for some species of cockroach to fully develop, while others mature in a matter of months. All roaches grow larger by molting their exoskeletons, and all of them reach a point when life slows down. They grow older, begin to stumble and trip on their own feet. They "dodder," as one observer put it. They lose the desire to get out and see the neighborhood, to explore. Their spontaneity dwindles, and they would rather just sit. By some estimates, a cockroach spends three-quarters of its life doing just that—sitting, observing, waiting, and hoping to avoid detection. To feel sorry for a cockroach is not my first inclination, but when I think about all that time alone, all that waiting around for nothing to happen, I can almost empathize.

One day when I was raking out in the backyard, grumbling to myself about the mess of weeds and rocks I didn't know what to do with, my new neighbor popped his head over the fence to introduce himself. Jack was a longtime resident of the neighborhood and had known the previous owners well.

"A shame," he said. "How fast they both went." He waved his pair of pruning shears in the air and explained how the wife had been taking care of her sickly husband for years and that everyone expected him to die first, but then she got sick herself.

"In six months, she was gone," Jack told me. "And in another six, so was he." Jack shook his head and stared at the house again. I told him about my family and our remodeling project and asked him about all the rocks in the yard.

"Used to be something," he said. "They spent all kinds of time out here. Had those rocks and a bench and some nice colored lights." He shrugged his shoulders. "But then they got sick and sort of let the whole thing go." I shook my head, and we talked a few more minutes about the house and the neighborhood, and then Jack turned back to his garden, leaving me to my rake and rocks.

We knew we wanted this house the moment our Realtor let us in the front door. In the past six months, we'd waded through the flotsam of the real estate market, cringing at the spoiled refrigerators, cracked-grout showers, and slanting floors that our price range had to offer, and we wondered how much mess and smell and work we could tolerate. During that first walk through the house, we'd mused about the old people that must have lived here—the old people who needed tape over the bathroom heater switch so they wouldn't leave it on and risk burning down the house; the old people who had a bath chair in their tub and a white spray nozzle hanging from the showerhead; the old people who'd left behind a hideous globular lamp hanging in the family room, its cord dangling loose like a hammock from the fixture head. The house had felt warm and even a little inviting then, as if it were waiting for us to move in, but talking with Jack that day in the backyard, I realized the house had also felt a little sad, as if it hadn't gotten used to being empty.

That day back in the title office, the old couple's daughter had told me about her husband, then just a teenager, pulling up in the driveway on weekend nights to drop her off after a date and how they would sit out in his car talking until her dad flicked the porch light, calling her in. How odd, I remember thinking then, to imagine someone else living in our house.

But now I keep imagining that father sitting in his recliner in our living room and waiting up for his daughter. He's reading the paper by the light of that awful yellow lamp, glancing occasionally at the clock on the wall, getting a bit nervous. His daughter had been a little girl in that home, too, wild and splashing in the bathtub and swinging from the trees in the back. She had a brother and a sister, and they would have been a tornado in the hallway, a blur of noise and teasing and growing like my boys are now, and all of the clatter and clang and life would have drained from the house slowly as the children grew up and moved out, leaving that father in his recliner with the newspaper folded in his lap and the lamp turned out for the night, no one left to wait up for.

A few days after we set out the traps, I saw a roach in the hall bathroom. He was smaller than the one Melissa caught in the kitchen, and he stood motionless near the corner by the door. He appeared frozen by the light, but I had the impression he was staring at me. Behind him, tucked between the wall and the door of the linen closet, sat a black roach motel. When I stood up, the roach didn't move. One quick step and I could have killed him, but I left him there unharmed, just a short crawl from what I hoped would be the last meal he'd ever find in our house.

I wonder about the old man's last night here in this house. Was that the night he died, or did the house sit empty while he moved away to expire in some hospital? I've thought about calling his daughter, but the idea feels tacky, intrusive, and self-serving. I don't want to bother her with my vain curiosity, to make her think about the new family living in her old home, to remind her that Melissa and I have been trying our best to scrub away all signs that her family ever lived here at all. She doesn't need to know that of all the memories kept alive by the presence of her mom and dad, the only ones that have persisted in their absence are the cockroaches.

The thing about vintage suits from the thrift store is this—the person who wore it last is probably dead, and more than likely, a moth has eaten a hole through one of the pockets.

Entomologists tell us that cockroaches have survived for 300 million years, that they've outlived dinosaurs, woolly mammoths, saber-toothed tigers, the dodo bird, and both my grandmothers. They tell us that roaches are an essential piece to a grand ecological puzzle in which no creature, no matter how disgusting, should be overlooked or demonized. They tell us that arthropods make up ninety percent of animal life on our small planet, and that society's preoccupation with cuddly looking vertebrates demonstrates our own higher-order arrogance. They tell us we have a lot to learn from these long-lived outcasts flicking their mandibles in the gritty shadows beneath the fridge. And to them, I say this: I'm the one with my name on the mortgage, the one paying the taxes, the one ripping up the old carpet and forever pulling weeds in the rocky backyard; I'm the one who's got to make this still-strange house into a place where I feel comfortable letting my sons scoot across the floor.

It had been early October when I spotted that first cockroach on the floor of my kitchen, and thanks in part to our well-placed traps and the numbing effect of a particularly cold winter, we hadn't seen one in months. Of course I knew they were out there, biding their time somewhere in the dark, waiting on the weather. But they'd largely dropped from my mind.

The old couple, though, kept cropping up everywhere, and some nights I would lie in bed, but sleep would not come for all the ghosts in the house. A hint of the wife in the kitchen as I pulled nails from the pantry wall. A specter of her husband as I rewired a broken switch to the rock-garden lights. Shadows of them both on each worn door panel, blackened from decades of fingers pressed against the wood. Sure, this was our house now, but it was their shag carpet still on the floor, their crumbs still buried in that carpet, and, of course, their cockroaches feeding on those crumbs. We signed the paperwork and inherited all of it, but I still felt like an unwelcome guest in my own home.

Then on a Saturday morning that first April, I opened my back door to take out the garbage and noticed in the slanting shadows of dawn small, green shoots breaking up out of the neglected flowerbeds around our back patio. I asked Melissa if she'd noticed them, and she pointed out four or five more shoots coming up in front of the house as well—happy green tips pointing up out of the soil.

Over the next few weeks, watching the progress of those perennials became a sort of game for the family, Melissa and I wondering what they might be—daffodils? lilies? tulips?—and the boys weeding out the soil around them, giving them space, keeping their feet and playground balls at a safe distance. When the shoots finally bloomed, the garden overflowed with deep-pink clusters of sickle-shaped petals—hyacinths that put a little blush on the cheeks of our sad backyard. How long ago had the old lady and her husband knelt down in the dirt to plant those flowers, turning over the late autumn soil, burying the bulbs deep against the winter, banking on the ancient promise of warm spring mornings? As the green world blossomed in our backyard, the flowers drew me outside more and more, and sometimes I stepped out to the patio just for the gift of it all: the leaves filling out the tree branches; the grass curling over the edge of the walk; the evening light bending around those pink flowers, offering the tiniest slivers of shadow on the ground. It was a spring shadow that I knew in the back of my mind would eventually call forth the roaches once more, a shadow that meant they were already on their way, a perennial reality that I could do little to stop.

I can almost see them now—our roaches, invigorated by spring and emerging from the darkness, lifting their olfactory receptors to the odor of the new family in the house. They move with a measure of patience and resignation available only to those whose evolutionary fight can be measured by the age of the earth. I call them our roaches, but as they slouch toward the house, I imagine their little steps sustained by the knowledge that they, the long-suffering roaches, are the ones who have inherited us.

Language Lust

Grit floors, grease, torn paper towels, condom vending machines, sticky toilet seats, and bathroom-stall graffiti. Dirty jokes and cuss words and racial slurs, male and female genitalia scratched into chipped paint, and phone numbers for "Tom" and "my ex-girlfriend" and "my roommate"—looking for a good time, cheap thrills, hot love. At a truck stop somewhere between Cheyenne and Indianapolis, in a bathroom stall like the inside of a teenage boy's mind, I leaned over to help my three-year-old son, Callan, wipe himself, grateful he could not read.

Almost as soon as I could read and write, I was passing notes. To the curly head in front of me, "Will you be my girlfriend?" To the blonde behind me, "Do you like me?" And to the brunette across the aisle, "Will you go out with me?" On the playground in first grade, my friends and I ran, half-heartedly, from the "Miss Kiss Club," a group of girls just learning the latent power of their lips, and that year I fell in love with Lisa McCracken. Other girls had inspired short notes, but Lisa deserved nothing less than a full-page love letter. "Dear Lisa," I must have started, and I remember writing several drafts, agonizing over my handwriting, struggling to convey my crush. And at some point, I know I wrote "I love you" because my older brother found a crumpled draft of the letter under my bed and for years taunted me to tears with the epithet "Lisa Lover."

In the library at my elementary school, across from the circulation desk, behind the pull-drawer card catalog, just out of the librarian's view, sat an oversized dictionary atop a wooden pedestal. Even at age seven, I could sense the reverence implied by the solitary podium and the weight of the open book it held—the call to worship, the temptation to defile. With the librarian out of sight, my friends and I opened the dictionary and pointed out words like *penis* and *sex* and then ran away giggling, afraid of being caught. At home, though, the game lost its charm, and I found myself, instead, turning the pages of my father's dictionary, scanning the pronunciation guides, reading definitions, admiring the occasional diagram, reveling in the heft and volume of my own language.

Spring of my sixth-grade year, I lay in the top bunk of a small, dark cabin filled with five other sixth-graders and our outdoor school counselor, Matt—a slightly overweight, bristly high-schooler who, even in his sleeping bag, wore the curved bill of his baseball cap low over his eyes. Our first night at camp and Matt was already telling dirty jokes, asking whether we knew any good ones. He asked us whether our mothers had caught us playing with ourselves and chuckled at some of the boys who said "no" before they realized their own confession. There was nothing elementary about the schooling he wanted to give us, and with all the warnings about sex and talking dirty I'd received at home and at church, I tried not to listen. Instead, I stared at the ceiling beams just above my head as Matt described various parts of his girlfriend's body, and I focused on what must have been decades of names and dates and initialed hearts cut into the wooden joists. Dozens, if not hundreds, of boys had slept in this bunk, carved their names in this wood, left a little piece of themselves behind. But I could not turn off my ears. All four nights, I stared at those names while Matt spoke in the dim light of the cabin, all the time feeling miles away from the innocent lust of kissing games and playground crushes. I felt relieved when his voice finally gave up each night, but I was permanently adrift, the feeling marked on the fourth and final night by a name and a date: Joey 04/93.

Walking down the aisle one day at Target with sixteen-month-old Callan sitting in the child restraint of the shopping cart, his little feet dangling in front of me, I noticed him craning his neck and twisting his torso to see in the direction we were heading. Unable to wiggle out of the safety strap and get himself turned around, he looked up at me frustrated and said, "Help-help." I turned the cart around and pushed from the front, giving him a clear view of the store as it unfolded before him. From this vantage point, he could see approaching shoppers, and, unaware of any taboos about calling out randomly to strangers, he waved his hands and said, "Hi" to everyone walking by. "Hi" to an old man shuffling behind his cart; "Hi" to the employee in the red polo bent over a box; and "Hi" to another baby bouncing on her father's shoulders. Most people responded with "how cute" or simply waved back. The more people responded, the more loudly and enthusiastically he called out to the people around him. More than one elderly woman stopped and held out a hand to pinch his cheek. One woman ran her finger slowly down the side of his face, studying him for a long time, unsure of what to think about this little boy, so willing to share his newly discovered language, so hungry for attention, so eager for approval.

Female approval was kind of a big deal in middle school—any female approval. I asked out fourteen girls in just two years. Four said yes, but the relationships went nowhere. A few furtive, flirtive phone calls, a note or two, hand-holding in the hallway, even occasional kisses. But after a short time, the relationships all ended. It was middle school, after all. No car, no cash, no courage. Some lasted only a week, and one less than a day.

Michelle was her name. I passed her a note in second period: "Will you go out with me?" Before third period, she approached me in the hallway, hugged me, and said, "Yes." After third period, she showed me her binder. In black ink she had written *JOEY* in large letters and encircled my name with hearts, swirls, and squiggles. She waved as she walked away to her next class, surrounded by her girlfriends. I didn't see her at lunch or during the last two periods of the day. When I did see her, it was right before I got on the bus to go home. "I can't go out with you anymore," she said over the giggling of her friends, and they walked away.

In high school, most people studied French, Spanish, and German—Romance languages for the normative student body, the beautiful masses, the cheerleaders and jocks and intellectuals. A disproportionate number of band geeks, drama nerds, and video-game fanatics took Japanese, along with a fair spattering of students like me who had no particular affinity for *Sailor Moon*, Final Fantasy, or Miyazaki films but were just looking for something different. So while my friends were learning *je ne c'est pas* from an ambiguously gay bachelor who showed us pictures from his summers spent in France with "a friend," *yo no sé* from a short Latina with a voice as big as her hair, and *ich weiss nicht* from Frau Freeman, whose name alone conjures crinkle skirts and frizzled blond hair, I was learning *wakiramasen* from a Sindhi expatriate raised in Japan and her teaching assistant, Mia Sensei. Beautiful Miss Mia. Twenty-one-year-old-out-of-reach-and-no-chance-even-if-I-were-her-age Miss Mia. At sixteen, knowing less about stereotypes of the Far East than I knew about Japanese syntax, I recognized something alluring in her quiet Asian coyness. If I'd known *Kubla Khan* back then, she would have been the Abyssinian maid, the damsel with a dulcimer, and I never would have approached her to save my life. Her quiet English gave her an air of mystery, made the possibility of contact doubly ridiculous, doubly fantastic. But I couldn't do anything except offer a shaky *konnichiwa* and a limp bow if we passed in the hallway.

Cara was an accidental girlfriend. A friend of a friend in high school, she sat at my lunch table one day and watched as I bummed change off everyone sitting around me and offered to make me lunch, which she did. Then I made her lunch, and then she made me lunch. By the end of the week, we were taking menu requests from each other, and our friends were talking, deciding what we were. We were okay *not* deciding. We were just friends, we said. Really. No benefits. I was graduating and going on a two-year church mission at the end of the summer, and we weren't interested in commitment. We played basketball, bought Slurpees and Mambas, hopped fully clothed into hotel pools, danced in public, watched movies, cooked for each other, and got into mock shouting matches that ended in fits of giggling. We were just friends, so leaving shouldn't have been a problem. But as my departure date loomed closer, we grew restless to define, solidify, and hold on to the summer—to each other. So on a Saturday afternoon, beneath sapling leaves, in the light of a hazy Oregon sunset, we did the only thing that seemed irrevocable, permanent, and promising—we carved our initials into a tree trunk: C+J.

Nathan wrote on the rocks. I couldn't believe it. Camped with our Boy Scout troop on a bed of pea-green moss, surrounded by sixty-foot-high evergreens, within earshot of a gurgling glacial stream, Nathan wrote in black Sharpie on dozens of smooth river stones sticking out of the ground near his tent. He wanted to be home with his girlfriend or playing his guitar, but his parents had made him come. And though I had wanted to leave him behind, we were Boy Scouts, and I wasn't the leader, so he came along. We were backpacking, and Nate wore a leather jacket and Doc Martens. He brought his gear in an old carry-on bag with a stiff plastic handle that rubbed his hands raw. His girlfriend, he told us during the hike, loved to hear him play his guitar, and she was going to help him start a band. Sometime after dinner, he slipped off to do his dirty work among the rocks: he drew band names; skulls; *NATE* in all caps; anarchy symbols with their circled, jagged A's; and his girlfriend's name in swooping, black flourishes. When he broke down his tent the next day, I followed behind him and turned the rocks over one by one, disrupting the soil in apology, trying to hide the truth that I'd helped bring him there.

"Play with me, Daddy," said Callan.

"Not now. I'm working."

"Pleeeeeeeease," he said.

"Why don't you color a picture?"

I brought out Callan's coloring book and a package of markers. He colored, and I went back to writing, back to worrying about telling "the truth" and corralling language and making meaning. When I got up to get a drink of water, I walked past Callan's work. He'd barely touched the page, but great swirls of color ran across the table, down its legs, and onto the palms of his hands.

As a child, I would occasionally ask a friend to hold out his hand, and then I would take it in mine and place two identical dots side by side on the back of his hand with my pen and ask, "What's the difference between these two dots?" When he answered that he didn't know, I would draw a line from one of the dots up his arm as far as I could and say, "This one's got a tail." The trick was to hold his hand tight so he couldn't pull it away until the pen line was going up his shirtsleeve. Dozens of times I played this trick on different friends, and each time the feeling of control, rather than intoxicating me, made me sick with guilt. "I'm sorry," I would say. "It will wash off."

Standing in the checkout line at a department store with my mom one day, probably buying deodorant, or Clearasil, or maybe even a new pack of underwear, I saw my Japanese teacher, Mrs. Bauman, walking toward me, followed closely by a few of the Japanese teaching assistants she worked with. Miss Mia may have been among them, which would have explained why, when they approached, I felt like I was standing there naked with my new underwear pulled over my head.

"*Konnichiwa, Joey-san,*" said my teacher. And then in Japanese, she asked me how I was doing. "*O genki desu ka?*"

I managed a fumbled reply—"*genki desu*"—but then she gave me a look that told me I'd forgotten something important. *Should I bow?* I thought, and I gave a little bow. I looked at Mrs. Bauman, who was still giving me the look. My eyes moved to the Japanese women smiling at her side, their black hair bobbed around their ears, their slight figures leaning forward, waiting for a proper greeting in their own language. My mind went blank.

"It's been . . . a long time . . . ," said my teacher under her breath in English, trying to jump-start my memory. I could hear the expression in my mind, could feel it floundering somewhere in the back of my mouth, but I could not make my tongue cooperate. And I still botched the phrase, *O-hisashiburi desu ne,* even after Mrs. Bauman repeated it for me twice. They said good-bye—in English—and walked away, leaving me holding my new pair of underwear, repeating the phrase over and over in my mind until it no longer sounded like language at all.

When my older brother Josh lost his job at Kinko's in 1997, he cashed in his last check on the way to 21st Century Tattoo in southeast Portland. He put the whole check—two hundred dollars—into a large, black Celtic knot that covered his entire left calf, a tessellation of intertwining rope that snaked over his skin, curling back on itself, disappearing and reappearing in a webbed pattern just visible above the top of his calf-high Doc Martens. When I asked him about it, he told me the knot was a "heritage piece," a nod to our Irish blood, now four generations thin, and I found myself surprised at the gesture. My brother—who had shocked me the first time he refused to pray at dinner, the first time he brawled with our father, the first time he brought home a copy of *Penthouse*, the first time he pierced an ear, the first time he talked openly about the drugs and sex of Portland counterculture—had in the most permanent ink, in the most unexpected way, embraced our family at its roots.

Coach Sheffield was a buffalo disguised as a PE teacher. His neck was as thick as his waist was as thick as his thighs, and his arms might as well have been thighs, too. He wore cotton-jersey shorts year-round that hugged his quadriceps, the leg hair exploding beneath the hemline and imploding again at the socks that covered his ankles—the only place he appeared skinny. In the winter he wore a black-and-orange windbreaker, and in the summer a white T-shirt that barely covered his shoulders. On his right triceps was the largest, most disturbing scar I have ever seen. Everyone knew it had once been a tattoo, and we knew we were supposed to notice it and learn from every ugly wrinkle. I used to imagine Coach as a younger man in his own youthful skin, the way he looked at it, the way he hoped a woman might look at it. I imagined him in the military or perhaps with a bunch of football buddies out for the weekend, drinking, talking tough, feeling stupid, and I thought of the nerve it would have taken to step through the doors of the tattoo parlor. What image would he choose? Was he trying to impress his buddies? A girl? Himself?

One day, while jogging around the football field with him, I asked about it.

"I got it in the navy," he said, looking straight ahead. "Stupidest thing I ever did."

As a somewhat athletic teenage boy with good grades and few skin problems, I managed through most of high school to survive near the upper end of the social food chain. However, teenage male prowess tends to relativity, which meant that in the locker room I slipped a few notches and that in my Japanese class I regained a little ground. So when Cory Brown—six-foot-four-inch-football-star-did-you-hear-he-did-pull-ups-hanging-from-the-overpass Cory Brown—walked into my Japanese class one day and lifted his shirt over his shoulders in front of the TA, Miss Mia, I was a little startled, a little jealous. The revelation of his bare back, all that smooth skin pulled taut over impossibly thick muscles curving as he leaned over and punctuated by a large black 死 freshly tattooed below his right shoulder, seemed to fill the room with testosterone. He was just a few inches from Miss Mia, and he was pointing at the black ink of the tattoo, still outlined in the tender redness of a fresh needle job, and she was startled—not repulsed but surprised in the way I imagine she was taught to be surprised, with one hand over her mouth, giggling, blushing. He pointed at the tattoo and said, "What does this mean?" And she giggled, and I couldn't help but think that she might want to reach out and touch the fresh tat, run her fingers across his back, and I felt like I'd just had the wind knocked out of me, like I'd just gotten a call from God to let me know that, sorry, the job of "Man" had been filled. And Miss Mia was still giggling, and Chris was still standing there, shirt over his shoulders, bare back exposed to the world, muscles bulging, the hot, black ink burning in his skin. "*Death*," she finally said. "That character means *death*." Then she burst into an ecstasy of giggling, and

Chris pulled his shirt down over his shoulders, satisfied, and walked out of the room.

I once watched Callan as he sat in our living room before an alphabet puzzle, trying to wrap his mind around the peculiar curve of the yellow wooden J in his hand. I watched him rotate, and test, and rotate again the small letter and then look up at me, eyes filled with his first questions of language and symbol. That was more than a year ago, and I see already the puzzle is getting more complex, more convoluted, and more compulsory—less innocent. At three, he is learning to write a few letters (C, A, L, and N), and he writes them down on loose papers, on his books, on our furniture, and he can't help but point them out in every street sign, billboard, and piece of junk mail he sees. It won't be long before he begins to put the entire alphabet together, before he reads everything, before symbols take over completely, before he begins to notice the sex and philosophy on a bathroom wall, on the playground, in the passing female figure, on the cluttered walls of his own mind. And the power of language and lust will give him the world but take something from him—prematurely, permanently, with no promise but to age him.

My Wife Wants You to Know
I'm Happily Married

The trick is to realize that one is not important, except insofar as one's example can serve to elucidate a more widespread human trait and make readers feel a little less lonely and freakish.
—Phillip Lopate, *The Art of the Personal Essay*

1.

A middle-aged man with a lumpy face and receding hairline stood at the pulpit. He introduced himself as a recent convert to our faith and a recent transplant from somewhere out of state, and then he gestured to his wife sitting in the back of the chapel and told us he was "married to the most beautiful woman in the world." For a split second, part of me thought, "Really? The most beautiful woman, here, in this room?" and I had the briefest of urges to turn around and see for myself. Of course I knew that line was just a sweet nothing—an offhanded, husbandly gesture meant to flatter, and I knew I shouldn't take him literally—but still, I was disappointed. Not in his wife's ordinary appearance, but in his lack of imagination—the way the line reduced his feelings about his wife to little more than a sales pitch—the cheap superlative of advertising hacks and political wonks. Love and attraction, it seems to me, are far more complicated and deserve a little more introspection.

At a recent minor league hockey game, I sat with my wife, Melissa, and our boys in the cheap section, while three teenage girls a few rows ahead of us stood on their seats, waving their rear ends at a television camera. These girls danced and laughed and craned their necks in hopes of seeing themselves on the giant screen hanging from the ceiling, looking, I imagine, for the high that comes from attention, even if that buzz is short-lived, and ironic, and merely feeding the arena's artificial energy—a false sense of excitement that required restoking every few minutes from the guys in the sound booth.

We were, after all, at a farm league hockey game in Salt Lake City (not exactly hockey country), and we were sitting in a small arena that was maybe half full, and most of us were there for the same reason—free tickets off the Internet. We did our part, though, as members of this artificial fan base and bought a six-dollar bag of popcorn before we sat down to watch the match. A few folks down the line were eating six-dollar hot dogs, one man had a six-dollar cardboard tray of nachos, and two men behind us were drinking eight-dollar pints of Coors Light and getting louder and louder as the match went on. We ate our popcorn and wiped our fingers on our napkins and dropped our salty kernels on the floor. Occasionally we glanced down at the men on skates flying around the rink, and if the arena ever got too quiet, a shrill voice came over the loudspeaker, urging us to "Make some noooise for your boooys!" despite the fact that few of us could have named a single player on the ice. Even the fight that broke out in the first three minutes of the game—complete with dramatic introductory gong ring courtesy of the guys in the sound booth—felt staged, one player screaming, throwing down his gloves, and lifting his fists in a "put up your dukes" gesture that drew a smirk from his would-be opponent. The players landed a few punches, and the more boisterous fans whistled and shouted, and some of them even put down their beers. But when a few punches turned into a scrum on the ice, and both players fell to the ground, the referees stepped in, and the two men swaggered off to their respective penalty boxes. The rest of the players got back to the business of running each other into the boards, some fans sat down, and some got up for more popcorn, and, I imagine, the producers in the sound booth gave each other high fives and then made a call to check on concession sales.

I teach young writers how to tell true stories, and we occasionally run up against the aesthetic question of hyperbole. Some students would play fast and loose with the truth. They think the "creative" in creative nonfiction gives them license to invent details out of whole cloth as long as they stay true to the "emotional truth" of their memories, whatever that means. But most students aren't looking to turn a traffic stop into a police chase or a hangnail into a tumor. Most students know they've lived relatively ordinary lives and are happy excavating those lives to share a bit of rough-polished humanity with someone else. They love Lopate's quote about feeling a little less lonely and freakish. But the question of hyperbole still remains—these stories we tell each other, no matter how close to the "truth," still rely on selective and often unreliable memory; they're still just snapshots that can never tell the whole experience. They're fish stories without witnesses. And even that photo you took to back up your fish story—the one with you and your dad posing along the river bank, that sliver of a trout dangling from a string, the two of you looking so happy, as if you did this sort of thing every day—even that photo is just another fish story.

What to do about hyperbole, though, when the fundamental unit of social currency is the story? What to do when all we've got to work with every day is the life we've lived and the body we were born into? We are all counterfeits and con artists in our own ways. Some of us tell first-date lies about where we work and why we're still living at home; some of us pad our résumés with fake degrees and fancy job titles or succumb to the lure of comb-overs, hair extensions, breast implants, or nose jobs; some of us line up for full-body wax treatments and spray-on tans. Viagra. Ritalin. Prozac. All just stories we swallow with a cold glass of water. Even the well-groomed lawn across the street, with its parallel tire stripes and hard-cut edges, is chapter one in a particular kind of story. We all have stories we hide behind, stories we crawl inside of, stories we order over the Internet and pay for on credit, stories we wish were true, stories we tell ourselves enough that we forget they are stories at all.

A fish story about my marriage: It was love at first sight. We've told it a thousand times, how we lived on opposite sides of Portland, Oregon, how at fifteen we met by chance at a church camp, and then how we didn't see each other for six long years until one fateful night at church where we met again; how we recognized each other right away, how our hearts skipped their respective beats. Melissa says, "I saw Joey, and I thought, 'Uh oh . . . here we go!'" and then, on cue, I say, "I knew it the moment I saw her." This is all true, of course, and yet I wonder how our story has been shaped by its outcome. After all, just because the planets seemed to align in our favor (her mother getting so sick that Melissa had to move back to Oregon at precisely the same time I moved back, both of us attending that same church meeting and then ending up at the same college living mere blocks from one another), no amount of coincidence means we were destined to be together. How different would my version of this story have been if we'd broken up after only a few weeks? Would it have been a story at all? Surely I would have met someone else, and together we would have aligned the planets in our favor. We would have identified all the signs that led our paths to cross, and we would have told our perfect story at dinner parties—and that story might have been the one on my mind when I sat down to write about hyperbole and relationships and this itch I've felt of late to stop telling myself so many stories.

2.

"My mistress' eyes are nothing like the sun," wrote Shakespeare in the most refreshing line of English poetry to come out of the sixteenth century. Sonnets blew up at the end of the 1590s "like rock 'n' roll in the '60s," according to a colleague of mine, and the shrapnel of that explosion included craggy chunks of hyperbole dripping with misogynistic admiration of the female form. Courtly poets heaped upon their readers the disembodied parts of their imagined lovers—eyes like diamonds or the sparkling heavens, noses like stately eagles, hair with "threads of finest gold," lips like cherries, teeth like pearls, necks like swans, even veins described as sapphires, and, thanks to Edmund Spenser, breath that smelled liked gilly flowers, goodly bosoms like beds of strawberries, and even nipples like blossomed jasmine. The scholar Jonathan Sawday describes these poets as engaging in a sort of poetic negotiation where "the female body was the currency," and the market hucksters trafficked in metaphoric one-upmanship. The Bard's 130th sonnet is, among other things, a reaction against this economy of "false compare" and suggests there's an element of dishonesty in such flowery praise, a paradoxical devaluing of true beauty through the hyperbolic assessment of its outward features, a cheap flower-and-candy gesture. In economic terms, these poets were cooking the books, printing their own money, hastening the inevitable collapse that is the natural result of unmitigated inflation.

I often teach an essay called "Live Nude Girl" by Kathleen Rooney. The essay's title instantly raises eyebrows with my students, and the persona on the page rarely disappoints. "I am twenty-five years old, five foot eight, 110 pounds, with huge dark eyes and long dark hair," she writes. "And I look totally f——ing amazing naked." This is a posture, of course—one that serves the essay well as it chronicles Rooney's adventures as a professional artist's model in New York City and also challenges readers' assumptions about nudity, privacy, and morality. With my students, I talk about Rooney's confident, in-your-face, and, well, naked persona, how it demands our attention and how she subtly undercuts that persona by meditating on her own self-consciousness, her hint of an eating disorder, her paradoxical acceptance of and resistance to being objectified, even by artists. The piece is beautifully wrought, and by the end of the class period, most students have embraced Rooney's persona completely. One semester, however, a student came to class the day after our discussion, and she raised her hand.

"So, I googled an image of Kathleen Rooney," she said. "And, well, I don't see what all the fuss is about."

My wife is not the most beautiful woman in the world. I've been told this is a dangerous thing to say, that I shouldn't let her hear that from me, that I'm asking for trouble (one female student looked so appalled when she heard me say this that you'd have thought I'd just admitted to cannibalism). But I don't see the issue. I'm hardly the most handsome man in the world (I've got hairy ears, a too-pointy chin, a joker's smile, and a blotchy red forehead when I laugh—I've been balding since my senior year of high school, for heaven's sake), and while I've heard all about "the eye of the beholder" and some abstract notions of "whole-package beauty," I can't help but see such comments as a posturing of sorts—not just false praise but an attempt to save face—as if the man at the pulpit in my congregation was trying to preempt anyone who might want to judge his wife on her looks. If that's true, then such a statement is less about how he sees his wife and more about how he wishes the world saw him.

For years, Melissa and I have had this joke in which one of us says, "Will you love me forever?" and the other says, "Of course I will."

"Even if my face gets scraped off?"

And then there's an uncomfortable pause before the other says something like, "What do you think?"

We laugh at this, but the chuckles always seem a bit self-conscious, perhaps because there's an insecurity we both feel about the faces we see in the mirror. Sure, I could love you in the event of some horrific accident, the joke insists. I could change the bandages and the sheets, empty the bed pans, rub ointment into the scars, caress the lips that are no longer lips. Ha ha ha, the joke says. Don't you know, silly, how much I love you? Really, the joke insists, I could do it. Couldn't I? Couldn't you?

3.

Much, I imagine, to Shakespeare's chagrin, the hyperbolic tendencies of most sixteenth-century sonnets are alive today in everything from Hallmark cards emblazoned with gold leaf and gaudy missives to reality TV shows that suggest true love can be narrowed down, one rose at a time, from a cast of jostling beauties. It's alive in the superfluity of glossy magazine articles about rock-hard abs, bikini-body workouts, and 101 ways to please your man; in romance novels about vampires and fetishism; and in pop songs about making love all night long.

I mean, really. Who wants to make love all night long?

A sports blog recently ran a post titled "5 Awesomely Terrible Hockey Romance Novel Titles." The author, Daniel Wagner, reports, "Today I discovered that there is such a thing as a hockey romance novel. I guess I shouldn't have been surprised. Romance novels are hugely popular among a certain subset of the population, and the same is true for hockey; those two worlds have to overlap somewhere." Wagner lists cheeky summaries of his favorite titles, which include gems, such as *Cross Check My Heart* (sexy physical therapist strikes up relationship with gritty league veteran); *Body Check* (determined publicist butts heads with the bad-boy team captain); and, my favorite, *Between a Jock and a Hard Place* (female pacifist accidently falls in love with league all-star).

I've never read a romance novel, let alone a hockey romance novel, but I'm not surprised by the formula, by the need for hero and heroine, lover and fighter, beauty and brawn, and the paradox of the romance genre that overstates the role of fate and chance in a relationship while simultaneously reducing the hard work of being in love to little more than submitting to sexual desire.

In high school, a girl we'll call Kate once tried to make peace after she'd broken up with me, after I'd already broken up with her. Yeah, it's as confusing as it sounds. There was, as there often is, another girl involved, as well as a ring (which is, perhaps, the high school definition of hyperbole). So Kate had given me a ring and then demanded it back, but then gave it to me again—a sort of self-righteous snub, her way of saying, "I'm still willing to be friends, despite what you did to me." Of course, as a sixteen-year-old romantic, I couldn't keep the ring, but I couldn't just throw it in the trash. The situation called for something dramatic—something out of a country music ballad.

That evening around sunset, I drove to our favorite park, walked out to our favorite wooden bridge, and looked out over the green water of our favorite suburban pond. I leaned against the wooden railing and tried to feel like a jilted lover. I held the cheap silver ring in my hand and tried to imagine a montage of our relationship together; I even tried to force some tears, but none came. Soon it grew so dark I could barely see the water beneath the bridge, and so, before the moment completely died, I reached back and let the ring fly into the water. I waited for the satisfying plunk to bring some closure, but the ring was too small and my throw too hard and the wind perhaps a little too strong, and the ring merely vanished into the dark.

"Beauty is truth, truth beauty," wrote Keats. "That is all ye know on earth, and all ye need to know," and that sounds pleasant enough, with its parallel structure and its subtle insistence on the primacy of the aesthetic experience, but I think it's possible that we don't trust the truth nearly enough, that instead we cling to what we think might pass for beauty. Perhaps that is why any public retelling of our story usually fails to include doubts Melissa and I both felt just a few months after our wedding, that hollow fear that we'd made a mistake, as if the rightness of our decision needed more validation than the fact that we'd made it, wide-eyed and hopeful. But doubt we did, and sometimes still do, based, I think, on an unhealthy assumption that out in the universe there lies some right path for us to walk, a story already written instead of one that is ours to create every time we rise with the sun.

A reality from our courtship: in February 2002 Melissa and I spent an evening together at the Salt Lake Winter Olympics. We sat close at a hockey match and strolled through the cosmopolitan crowds of Olympic Park. The night was clear and unseasonably warm, and the bright lights of the city blinked overhead. We were on that magical date when a couple is supposed to realize they want to spend the rest of their lives together, except that the night was wholly and completely ordinary. Not bad, but nothing to write home about either. I can't even remember who won the hockey match, or who played, or what we talked about. We would be engaged by summer, and looking back on this night, it could have been an important landmark on our way to the altar, but the truth of that night, no matter how I might romanticize the evening, is this: We were comfortable in the most mundane way possible, as much friends as lovers, and we spent a forgetful evening under the lights of a billion-dollar sporting extravaganza and then ended the evening hungry and uncomfortable, falling asleep on the bus ride back home.

4.

I remember sitting in Psych 110 my first semester in college and staring at two composite images of men in my textbook. One image was an amalgam of "masculine" features—angular jaw, facial stubble, and pronounced cheekbones—and the other was a composite of what we might call "softer" features. The book explained that the average ovulating woman will be attracted to the more masculine composite, while women in other stages of the menstrual cycle will be attracted to the less masculine. But that's not all, I've discovered. An ovulating woman can actually smell whether a man's facial features are more symmetrical than another's, and if she's currently in a relationship with a partner who falls into the "soft features" category, a woman is more likely to let her eyes wander during ovulation. And finally, men tend to find ovulating women more attractive—a penchant with obvious evolutionary advantages. What does all this mean? I'm not sure, exactly, but it does seem to suggest that no matter how much a particular person strikes our fancy, our bodies are, at least on the cellular level, only interested in the hard truth of cold chemistry.

I'm six feet tall with my shoes on, but I never put that down on a form that wants to know how tall I am. I round down because the idea of compensating on paper seems more emasculating than saying five eleven. I keep my hair cut short for similar reasons—I don't want anyone to think I'm in denial about losing my hair. These are moments of modesty for which I congratulate myself. But even if I no longer worry about the hair growing on my shoulders the way I did as a teenager, I still pluck whiskers out of my nose and ears when I notice them, and I still suck in my gut when I catch my reflection in a window. In many ways, I still feel like the insecure teenager who, a few months after dropping off the high school football team, signed up for a gym membership and sheepishly gave this answer when the personal trainer asked for my workout goals: "I, uh, well . . . I want to look good at the beach." This inner teenager has joined a handful of gyms over the years and puts in a few ambitious months of treadmill and weight-machine work here and there, but I like to think I've mostly outgrown him. After all, I'm a full-blown adult with cholesterol to worry about, and the dangers of belly fat, and my doctor's mantra about the long-term benefits of cardiovascular exercise ringing in my ears—plenty of reasons to go to the gym. And yet my inner teenager knows the real reason I go, if I go at all. I'm thirty-four years old, a father of three, and a college professor, but I'm still worried about that first summer day when I've got to put on a swimsuit.

I was once friends with a three-hundred-pound hula instructor from Hawaii who told me that back home her nickname was "Kanak Attack"—a Hawaiian phrase that means "eat until you drop." One afternoon, over lunch, she told me she didn't care what her husband looked like as long as he was a good man. "We'll all look good in heaven," she told me. "I can wait."

Occasionally, people have told Melissa she looks like Uma Thurman (a celebrity who, incidentally, ranks high on at least one of those "most beautiful women in the world" lists), and at times I can see the resemblance—same high forehead, same olive-shaped eyes, same cheekbones with a blend of curves and lines that shift according to the camera's angle of approach. And I know Melissa has felt flattered by the comparison in the same way that I felt flattered once when someone told me I looked like the TV actor Joel McHale. But such comparisons always leave me a little uncomfortable, at least in part because of social expectations associated with Hollywood beauty and for the inevitable end to such a comparison: the "yeah, I can kinda see that, but ..." that follows an online image search of Uma Thurman or Joel McHale. (Perhaps I could have passed for McHale during his pre-hair-plugged Seattle improv days, but not today.)

This comparison is unfair, of course. It demands we explain beauty as a relational thing, as if such hierarchy matters in our day-to-day romances, as if a rose in the garden makes the daisy less a wonder, as if a sunset in Hawaii ruins one in Utah. But if we are making comparisons, consider this: Joel McHale has much more reason than I do to put in time at the gym (and at the Hair Club for Men), and Uma Thurman has hair dressers, stylists, publicists, and personal trainers who get paid to help her look amazing. Still, the tabloid celebrity personas they both work so hard to cultivate are, I imagine, no more a complete picture of either of them than is any snapshot of me and the backside of my head, or of my wife in her sweatpants while she's dragging our boys through the grocery store on her way to a hair appointment at Fantastic Sam's.

In our first ten years of marriage, the joke about getting our faces scraped off has had remarkable staying power, the way tired jokes do in a happy relationship. But then a few years ago, our friend's sister and her husband were in an airplane crash in St. Johns, Arizona. Stephanie and Christian Nielson had just taken off with their pilot when something went wrong, and the plane crash-landed in a neighborhood near the airport. All three managed to pull their burning bodies from the wreckage, but the pilot died shortly afterward in the hospital, and Stephanie and Christian found themselves in medically induced comas—Christian for several weeks and Stephanie, with burns on 80 percent of her body, for three months. Their children waited with relatives to see if Mom and Dad would survive. News outlets picked up their story, and Stephanie's sister gave a play-by-play on her blog, where Melissa and I followed their recovery.

We read of the surgeries and the skin grafts and the pain of trying to stitch Stephanie's body back together and of trying to reconstruct her face, which had all but burned away in the flames. We read about Christian visiting Stephanie's room every day, and we read about Stephanie waking up and turning the corner from survival to recovery. We read about them starting over as a family, about their children's fear of Mom's scarred face, about Stephanie's persistent anxiety over her ability to return to life as a mother and wife. We read about their rekindled romance and how they began to see every day with each other and their children as a gift. Their story made it onto the morning talk shows, and Oprah, and eventually onto the pages of a memoir. Along with millions of people around the country, Melissa and I stood on the sidelines, in awe of the tragedy and the miracle, and we marveled without irony at the clichés they were proving true—notions of the human spirit and its power, of love conquering all, of true definitions of beauty. We juxtaposed our own supposed challenges with theirs and sensed that we had a lot to learn, that we had little to complain about, and that jokes involving faces getting scraped off were, at second glance, not as funny as we had supposed.

5.

A nihilist will tell you that consciousness itself is hyperbole—
that you and I are little more than sweaty animals burrowing
into our own corners of the world. Humanity is an overstate-
ment, a fiction—albeit a necessary one—that keeps us from
succumbing to our own Darwinian dispositions. But I think
such Nietzschean pronouncements are a sort of hyperbole
in their own right, spoken, perhaps, in fear of the collective
responsibility that comes from the audacious claim that you
and I are actually more than just animals. And I think such
pronouncements echo the oft-made claim that all writing is
fiction. It takes courage to suggest that we are more than beasts
and that we have a responsibility to one another, and it takes
courage to suggest that we are more than just storytellers and
that we have a responsibility to the truth.

A few weeks after attending that minor league hockey game,
Melissa and I took our boys to an unadorned ice rink at the edge
of town to watch a pair of college hockey teams in a midseason
match. We joined a few hundred other fans on the aluminum
bleachers and watched the teams warm up on the ice. Where
the minor league players we'd watched a few weeks back had
fluttered onto the ice like a flock of preening peacocks, these
two underfunded club teams took to the ice with their heads
down and little more than pride at stake. The PA system—with
its playful music and enthusiastic MC that would have made
the game feel a bit festive—was on the fritz, and so instead we
heard only the grunting of players, the chopping of sticks, the
vibration of boards and Plexiglas, and the shudder of our own
collective gasps. We watched the two teams slap, push, trip, and
beat up on each other without throwing a single blow, except
once, when an enforcer from the opposition sucker-punched a
home-team defender while the referees weren't looking. The

kid hit the ice, and the crowd gasped, and a few diehard fans in the front row jumped from their seats like chained dogs. There was no excitement in the crowd, only the cold taste of blood, and I wanted to tell my boys to avert their eyes. I remember thinking, if hockey has a pure, unadulterated core, then this is it, and it felt that night as if the ice might crack from the weight of it.

I admire the way a haiku poet can find heft in the simplest of images, writing the world exactly as it appears, overcoming what Pound described as the impasse between what we feel and what we can express—an impasse that often leads to hyperbole in the less patient among us, poets and plebeians alike. In the haiku of Bashō, I find the frankness I appreciate in Shakespeare:

> Among moon gazers
> at the ancient temple grounds
> not one beautiful face

and I hear the subtle appreciation of beauty I hope to cultivate in my own relationship:

> Wrapping dumplings in
> bamboo leaves, with one finger
> she tidies her hair

and I sense a desire to feel a little less lonely:

> This bright harvest moon
> keeps me walking all night long
> around the little pond

And while walking all night long around a pond may be a bit on the hyperbolic end of the haiku spectrum, even for a poet famous for walking, it is at least more plausible than making love all night long.

Stephanie and Christian Nielson's public story of their private anguish is startling and inspiring, and yet I don't think it's the most remarkable part of their story. Certainly the intimate details of their tragedy are moving, and they have invited the world in to get a hint at what it has been like to rebuild their lives together after the plane crash. But the remarkable part to me is that outside of the camera's view, off the pages of their memoir, and beyond the reach of the interviewer's microphone, they are just another family, eating meals together, discussing school assignments and vacation plans, attending soccer games, and dressing up for Halloween. They fight and disagree and tire of each other, and they make up and make love and make plans for the future, just like any of us. Their dance with death and the graceful way they came out of it fixed them for a moment in the public eye and defined them for millions of people. But in the end, the story they've chosen to tell renders the accident as just another chapter, and while it has certainly changed everything, ultimately, at the core of their relationship, it appears to have altered nothing.

Truth and Beauty are at the heart of every relationship: the question of what happened and how to frame it. On the one hand, it might be said that we are a meaning-making species, and so whatever beauty we find in the stories we tell each other is truth enough. But on the other hand, it is possible that truth is more beautiful when given a chance to stand for itself. And this is the paradox and genius of the essay. It can only be a distortion of the truth, an overemphasis on particulars, a privileging of one persona over so many others. But in that disembodied partial sampling of the writer's life, we begin to see a glimpse of who the writer really is, and, in turn, we see that for all our own freakishness, we are relatively normal.

Nearly every fall during graduate school, Melissa threatened to make me a shirt that read, "My wife wants you to know that I am happily married." I always interpreted the joke as flattery and maybe a little understated concern about the prospect of someone hitting on me during a class or study session, but just recently I've imagined a third interpretation. What if such a shirt was not designed to ward off a harmless flirt or a would-be seductress but instead was meant to remind me, the wearer, of a particular version of our story. What if it was not merely a label that said "Mine" but a note that meant "Don't forget"? This is, after all, the big question of marriage: not whether the truth will always be beautiful but whether we can remember moments of beauty when the truth is anything but. I think it's possible that the story of every good marriage is built on this kind of hyperbole, a series of well-spun yarns that remind us why we're together, that help us reaffirm we've made the right choice—that the person we wake up to each morning is really the person we want to wake up to.

Psychologists call this confirmation bias.

Poets call it being in love.

I am not a journalist. Nor am I a psychologist, historian, ethnographer, criminologist, entomologist, art critic, linguist, or neuroscientist, and I make no claim to an expertise in any of these fields nor in the handful of other areas in which I dabble as part of this collection. Rather, these humble offerings are little more than experiments on my experience, each one a trial of my thoughts, a "loose sally of the mind," as Samuel Johnson calls them. I have as often as possible sought the opinions of better-trained minds to help validate these experiments and have included these notes in order to give credit where credit is due.

And when I've had only myself to go on, I have, as Dinty W. Moore suggests we should, "done my darndest" to get the details right. I have changed a few names in the interest of privacy, but the people, places, events, and chronologies recorded here are as close to accurate as I could get them in the service of each essay, and while there surely are mistakes, errors, omissions, and oversights in this collection, they are accidental, incidental, and, I hope, inconsequential to your reading experience. Cheers!

The Lifespan of a Kiss

I owe it to Christopher Nyrop and the English translation of his 1901 book-length essay, *The Kiss and Its History,* for getting me started on the path that ultimately led to this essay. He turned me on to the story of Francesca and Paolo and introduced me to the words of Socrates on kissing and to Lord Byron's obsession with it. Anyone looking for an erudite and clever treatment of kissing that spans from the nineteenth century back to antiquity should read Nyrop's book. But remember his warning.

In addition to Nyrop, I have relied on a variety of sources, literary and otherwise, to help get the facts straight in this meandering, somewhat haphazard project on kissing, and to them I am grateful. As for the Marilyn Monroe quote, it's all over the Internet and on a few e-books, but it doesn't show up in any of her major biographies as far as I can tell, so it may require an asterisk of sorts.

Alighieri, Dante. *The Divine Comedy*. Trans. Henry Francis Cary. Chicago: Thompson & Thomas, 1901. *Project Gutenberg*.

Byron, George Gordon, Lord. *Don Juan*. Halifax: Milner and Sowerby, 1837. *Project Gutenberg*.

Chadwick, Henry, ed. *Spalding's Baseball Guide and Official League Book for 1895*. New York: American Sports Publishing Co, 1895. *Project Gutenberg*.

Chekhov, Anton. *The Kiss and Other Stories*. Trans. Ronald Wilks. New York: Penguin Classics, 1982.

Conway, Kelley. *Chanteuse in the City: The Realist Singer in French Film*. Berkeley: University of California Press, 2004.

Cummings, E. E. "Since Feeling Is First." In *100 Selected Poems*. New York: Grove Press, 1994.

Goldman, William. *The Princess Bride*. Orlando: Harcourt, 2003.

McLelland, Mark. "'Kissing Is a Symbol of Democracy!' Dating, Democracy, and Romance in Occupied Japan, 1945–1952." *Journal of the History of Sexuality* 19.3 (2010): 508–35.

Nyrop, Christopher. *The Kiss and Its History*. Trans. William Frederick Harvey. Detroit: Singletree Press, 1968.

Pride and Prejudice. Dir. Joe Wright. Perf. Keira Knightley, Matthew Macfadyen, and Brenda Blethyn. Focus Features, 2005.

Richie, Donald. *A Lateral View: Essays on Culture and Style in Contemporary Japan*. Berkeley: Stone Bridge Press, 1992.

TLC. "Virgin Couple Shares First Kiss—Virgin Diaries." Youtube.com.
    Uploaded November 29, 2011.

In addition, I owe an enormous debt of gratitude for the precise interpretations of Rodin's life and work that were found in the biographies and monographs below. I could not have spoken with any confidence about Rodin without leaning on these fine scholars.

Busco, Marie. *Rodin and His Contemporaries*. New York: Cross River
    Press, 1991.
Butler, Ruth. *Rodin: The Shape of Genius*. New Haven: Yale University
    Press, 1993.
Crone, Rainer, and Siegfried Salzmann, eds. *Rodin: Eros and Creativity*.
    Munich: Prestel, 1992.
Grunfeld, Frederic V. *Rodin*. New York: Henry Holt, 1986. Print.
Elsen, Albert E. *The Gates of Hell by Auguste Rodin*. Stanford: Stanford
    University Press, 1985.

Grand Theft Auto

During multiple phone conversations, Officer Robert Filar of the Athens Police Department supplied me with some of the details about the history of the man who stole my car and explained the events of his arrest. Despite the blur of that twenty-four-hour period, I did my best to remember those conversations, but I may have misunderstood some of the facts. However, since the essay is specifically about imagining what happened and not about what actually happened, I hope readers will accept the "facts" of this story in that spirit.

Climbing Shingle Mill Peak

Milligan, Mark. "What are those lines on the mountain? From bread
    lines to erosion-control lines." *Survey Notes* 42.1 (January 2010). Utah
    Geological Survey. geology.utah.gov.

Thoreau, Henry David. *Walden, Or, Life in the Woods.* New York: Times Mirror, 1963.

"The Fourth World Jamboree," *Scouting History Around the Globe.* usscouts.org.

On Haptics, Hyperrealism, and Prison

Bastian, Heiner, ed. *Ron Mueck.* London: Hatje Cantz, 2006.

Bush, Elizabeth. "The Use of Human Touch to Improve the Well-Being of Older Adults: A Holistic Nursing Intervention." *Journal of Holistic Nursing* 19 (2001): 256–71.

Fisher, Jeffrey D., Marvin Rytting, and Richard Heslin. "Hands Touching Hands: Affective and Evaluative Effects of an Interpersonal Touch." *Sociometry* 39.4 (1976): 416–21.

Hertenstein, Matthew J., et al. "The Communicative Functions of Touch in Humans, Nonhuman Primates, and Rats: A Review and Synthesis of Empirical Research." *Genetic, Social, and General Psychology Monographs* 132.1 (2006): 5–94.

Hurlston, David, ed. *Ron Mueck.* New Haven: Yale University Press, 2011.

Jansson-Boyd, Catherine V. "Touch Matters: Exploring the Relationship between Consumption and Tactile Interaction." *Social Semiotics* 21.4 (2011): 531–46.

Joule, R.V., and N. Guéguen. "Touch, Compliance and Awareness of Tactile Contact." *Perceptual and Motor Skills* 104 (2007): 581–88.

Kaufman, Douglas, and John M. Mahoney. "The Effect of Waitresses' Touch on Alcohol Consumption in Dyads." *The Journal of Social Psychology* 139.3 (1999): 261–67.

Miller, Susanna. "Memory in Touch." *Psicothema* 11.4 (1999): 747–67.

Rubinkam, Michael. "Pa. Widow Builds Vault, Could Get Corpses Back." *San Diego Union-Tribune.* Web. January 4, 2011.

———. "Widow Lives with Corpses of Husband, Twin." *The Boston Globe.* Web. July 5, 2010.

Houseguest

After I got over my disgust for the cockroaches that had made such a long and thorough infestation of my new home, my curiosity gradually took over, and I owe everything I have learned about them to several books and websites dedicated to the underappreciated insects. In particular, I owe the idea of roaches as being "uncharismatic" to Bell, Roth, and Nalepa, whom I paraphrase in this essay. Their original line, "Cockroaches are not generally considered a charismatic taxon; species that are threatened with extinction are unlikely to rally conservationists to action" (173), is so wonderfully deadpan in its understatement that it deserves noting here.

Bell, William J., Louis M. Roth, and Christine A. Nalepa. *Cockroaches: Ecology, Behavior, and Natural History*. Baltimore: Johns Hopkins University Press, 2007.

Copeland, Marion. *Cockroach*. London: Reakton Books, 2003.

Evans, Howard E. "The Intellectual and Emotional World of the Cockroach." *Harper's* 233.1399 (December 1966): 50–55.

Miall, L. C., and Alfred Denny. *The Structure and Life-History of the Cockroach*. London: Lovell Reeve & Co., 1886. Web.

"Sex Hungry Roaches Lured to Death." BBC *News*. Web. Friday, February 18, 2005.

My Wife Wants You to Know

Much thanks to Rick Duerden and Nancy Christiansen for their knowledge of Shakespeare and for introducing me to the critical conversation surrounding blazons (the poetic category of those sixteenth-century over-the-top love poems Shakespeare had such a problem with). Bonus points if you can find the unintended pun in this essay based on that word. Seriously though, locate the pun, and if you send me the correct answer along with a self-addressed, stamped envelope, I'll send you a personalized blazon poem written on your behalf to any object of your affection, human or otherwise.

And the censored f-word that appears in a quote in this chapter—that was my doing. I figure two em-dashes are simpler that trying to explain to my boys why Dad's book has the f-bomb in it. Nolan came home from preschool one day repeating that word over and over again, but that was five years ago, and I think he's forgotten it. I don't want to be the one to remind him.

I am also indebted to Shambhala Press for permission to republish a few of Sam Hammill's elegant translations of Bashō's poetry (see full acknowledgment in the front of the book), and to the authors of the following sources.

Gangestad, Steven W., Randy Thornhill, and Christine E. Garver-Apgar. "Men's facial masculinity predicts changes in their female partners' sexual interests across the ovulatory cycle, whereas men's intelligence does not." *Evolution and Human Behavior* 31 (2010): 412–24.

Lopate, Phillip. "Introduction." *The Art of the Personal Essay*. New York: Anchor, 1994.

Rooney, Kathleen. "Live Nude Girl." *Twentysomething Essays by Twentysomething Writers*. New York: Random House, 2006.

Thornhill, Randy, and Steven W. Gangestad. "The Scent of Symmetry: A Human Sex Pheromone that Signals Fitness?" *Evolution and Human Behavior* 20 (1999): 175–201.

In the American Lives Series

Turning Bones
by Lee Martin

In Rooms of Memory: Essays
by Hilary Masters

Between Panic and Desire
by Dinty W. Moore

Sleep in Me
by Jon Pineda

Works Cited: An Alphabetical
Odyssey of Mayhem
and Misbehavior
by Brandon R. Schrand

Thoughts from a Queen-Sized Bed
by Mimi Schwartz

My Ruby Slippers: Finding Place
on the Road Back to Kansas
by Tracy Seeley

The Fortune Teller's Kiss
by Brenda Serotte

Gang of One: Memoirs
of a Red Guard
by Fan Shen

Just Breathe Normally
by Peggy Shumaker

Scraping By in the Big Eighties
by Natalia Rachel Singer

In the Shadow of Memory
by Floyd Skloot

Secret Frequencies: A
New York Education
by John Skoyles

The Days Are Gods
by Liz Stephens

Phantom Limb
by Janet Sternburg

Yellowstone Autumn: A Season of
Discovery in a Wondrous Land
by W. D. Wetherell

To order or obtain more information on these or other University of Nebraska Press titles, visit nebraskapress.unl.edu.